THE KNIGHTS
TEMPLAR

A SECRET HISTORY

GRAEME DAVIS

First published in Great Britain in 2013 by Osprey Publishing,
Midland House, West Way, Botley, Oxford, OX2 0PH, UK
44–02 23rd St, Suite 219, Long Island City, NY 11101, USA

E-mail: info@ospreypublishing.com

Osprey Publishing is part of the Osprey Group
© 2013 Osprey Publishing

The Publisher has made every attempt to secure the appropriate permissions for material
reproduced in this book. If there has been any oversight we will be happy to rectify the situation
and written submission should be made to the Publishers. All uncredited images are assumed to be
in the public domain.

A CIP catalog record for this book is available from the British Library

Print ISBN: 978 1 78200 409 7
PDF e-book ISBN: 978 1 4728 0646 8
EPUB e-book ISBN: 978 1 4728 0647 5

CONTENTS

Introduction

The death of Dr Émile Fouchet in the spring of 2012, in an automobile accident outside Troyes, excited little comment. The police report concluded that Dr Fouchet had been drinking but was not drunk, and that darkness and rain contributed to the crash. The question of suicide, prompted by the recent and unexpected loss of his teaching post at the University of Toulouse, was raised and quickly dismissed.

I had met Dr Fouchet briefly at the International Congress on Medieval Studies in 2007. He gave a paper tracing the history of what he called the "Plantard conspiracy"[1] which lay behind *The Da Vinci Code* – wildly popular at that time – and the 1982 bestseller *The Holy Blood and the Holy Grail*. The topic seemed too lightweight for an academic conference, but Fouchet's presentation posed several intriguing questions. In particular, while dismissing the books and film as blatant fiction, he wondered who would spend so much effort to obfuscate historical facts, and why.

After his presentation I took the opportunity to request Dr Fouchet's help for one of my graduate students who was researching links between the Templars and the Teutonic Knights. I also made some politely noncommittal remarks about his choice of topic and his courage in broaching it before an academic audience. He complimented me on my French and promised to read my student's abstract.

Nothing in our conversation made me think Dr Fouchet would remember me once he was out of the room. His letter in response to the abstract was polite but distant. He listed some archives and the names of a few librarians, but regretted that he was extremely busy with his own research.

Shortly after Fouchet's death I received a package. Inside was a mass of papers and a letter dated three days before the crash. Fouchet had apparently kept up with my work and seemed impressed by my publication record, for his letter begged me to have his research translated and published as quickly as possible if anything should happen to him. He sounded very afraid – almost paranoid – and hinted that his recent research had cost him his job and somehow placed him in danger.

In 2006, construction work on a new Metro station in Toulouse uncovered part of the ruined Château Narbonnaise. Also found, though not reported,

---

1. Although it dates back to the 1950s, the Plantard conspiracy came to worldwide prominence following the publication of *The Holy Blood and the Holy Grail* in 1982. It is covered in more detail on pp. 61-62.

was a cache of documents dating from the siege of the castle in 1217-18 during the Albigensian Crusade.

The documents were mostly religious and philosophical texts relating to the Cathar heresy, and Fouchet was an expert on Cathar history. As he studied the documents he found some relating to the Knights Templar, who survived the Albigensian Crusade but were disbanded about a century later.

I spent the whole of that night poring over Fouchet's notes. At first I suspected Fouchet had fallen prey to the kind of conspiracy theories that have always dogged serious Templar scholarship. To my surprise I found Fouchet's facts unassailable, his arguments sound, and his tone manifestly sane. I decided to do as he asked, and you hold the first results of that process in your hands. It is hoped that deeper and more detailed coverage of Fouchet's research will appear over the next few years in peer-reviewed journals.

One sentence in Fouchet's letter still puzzles me. "You must publish," he said, "before they can cover the old fiction with a new one." If "they" are the Templars, or some group claiming the inheritance of their legacy, then it seems the "Plantard conspiracy" – and other Templar myths – were deliberate and well-constructed fictions.

For now, readers must come to their own conclusions and hope, as I do, that someone with the necessary expertise and resources will take up the research that Émile Fouchet can no longer finish.

JACQUES DE MOLAY, chef des Templiers

Jacques de Molay, last official Grand Master of the Knights Templar. In the absence of convincing contemporary likenesses, this later image has become the most influential depiction. (Mary Evans Picture Library / Alamy)

Origins and Growth

The history of the Knights Templar, from their founding in 1119 to the execution of the last Grand Master, Jacques de Molay, in 1314, is sufficiently well known that it need only be covered here in outline. More details can be found in many excellent sources, some of which are listed in the bibliography.

In addition to the generally accepted history of the Order, the following pages also discuss various points raised in Fouchet's notes, and the startling conclusions he drew from his research.

The Founding

In July of 1099 the armies of the First Crusade captured Jerusalem, bringing the Holy Lands of the Middle East under Christian control after more than 450 years of Muslim domination. Around 1119 nine French knights, including Hugues de Payens, André de Montbard, and Godfrey de Saint-Omer, approached King Baldwin II of Jerusalem with a proposal to establish an order of knights on monastic lines, whose duty would be to protect pilgrims as they traveled to Jerusalem.

The knights were accommodated in the captured al-Aqsa Mosque on the Temple Mount, close to the site of Solomon's Temple. They named themselves the "Poor Knights of Christ and the Temple of Solomon," which soon became abbreviated to "Knights of the Temple" or "Knights Templar."

Pope Honorius II presides over the Order's official foundation at the Council of Troyes. (INTERFOTO / Alamy)

Their fame spread to Europe, where they returned in 1127 to a heroes' welcome. Leading churchman Bernard (later Saint Bernard) of Clairvaux became their champion, writing *De Laude Novae Militae* ("In Praise of the New Knighthood") and playing a leading role in the 1128 (1129 according to some sources) Council of Troyes at which Pope Honorius II gave their order official status. Hugues de Payens was established as the Templars' first Grand Master.

After this official recognition gifts of money and lands poured in, along with a flood of eager recruits. The Order was further strengthened in 1139 by a bull of Pope Innocent II titled *Omne Datum Optimum* ("Every Perfect Gift"), which exempted members of the Order from the laws of the kingdoms in which they operated. They could pass freely across borders, were exempt from taxation, and answered only to the pope. No king could command the Templars.

Contemporary Records

Guillaume de Tyre, our main source for the Templars' early history, was born more than a decade after the Order was allegedly founded. When he was writing, between 1170 and 1184, the Templars were already well established and influential.

Bernard was given the Abbey of Clairvaux by Count Hugh of Champagne, the head of the Troyes cabal. (INTERFOTO / Alamy)

King Baldwin's own chronicler was his chaplain Fulk, or Fulcher, de Chartres. Fulk himself does not even mention Hugues de Payens. This is curious, as Fulk would surely have witnessed his master's meeting with the nine poor knights.

In fact, nowhere in the records of the time is there any mention of de Payens and his knights being active in the Holy Land. Even the later accounts fail to record any action in which they protected pilgrims. One must wonder how nine impoverished knights could hope to protect so many travelers in such a large area; so far no one has been able to answer this question.

According to Fouchet, the story of the nine poor knights seems less like history and more like a *post facto* origin story fabricated for an organization that already existed.

King Baldwin grants accommodations in the Temple to Hugues de Payens and Geoffrey de Saint-Omer. From a 13th-century copy of Guillaume de Tyre's *Histoire d'Outre-Mer.* (PD-US)

The Troyes Connection

Hugues de Payens was a vassal of Count Hugues (Hugh) of Champagne. The count endowed the abbey of Clairvaux and installed Bernard as abbot. Bernard was a nephew of André de Montbard, de Payens' companion. The counts of Champagne made their capital at Troyes, where the Church council that officially recognized the Templars took place. Fouchet believed that this is more than mere coincidence.

In 1104, more than a decade before the Templars were officially founded, Count Hugh met with certain nobles, at least one of whom had recently returned from Jerusalem. That same year, the count set out on a four-year journey to the Holy Land in the company of Hugues de Payens.

De Payens was more than just a vassal to Count Hugh. His signature appears on several of the count's documents, suggesting that he was a trusted courtier and possibly a friend.

There is no official record of what de Payens and his lord did in the Holy Land. It is known, however, that in 1114 Count Hugh made a second journey there, again with de Payens. A letter from Bernard refers to the count's desire to join *la milice du Christ* – the name was often applied to the Templars, but they would not be founded for another five years. "The Militia of Christ" was a completely new term, but Bernard used it as though it were quite familiar to him.

Count Hugh returned to France within a year, leaving de Payens behind. Almost as soon as he returned, he gave land to the Cistercians for the building of Clairvaux Abbey. Bernard, who was only 25 and had been a Cistercian for just three years, was installed as abbot.

Count Hugh joined the Order in 1124, swearing fealty to de Payens as the Order's Grand Master – and placing himself in the anomalous position of vassal to his own vassal.

The counts of Champagne who followed Hugh were frequent visitors to the Holy Land. One, Henry II, was king of Jerusalem from 1192 to 1197 and died in suspicious circumstances. In 1198, Pope Innocent III chose Count Tibault (or Theobald) of Champagne to lead the Fourth Crusade and recapture Jerusalem.

Fouchet's research included an exhaustive enquiry into Count Hugh and his successors. He also tried to trace the other members of what he called "the Troyes cabal" and chart their connection with the Templars and the kings of Jerusalem. The fact that he died near Troyes suggests that someone – or some organization – wanted to stop his enquiries into events there.

What does emerge from Fouchet's research is the idea that as early as 1104 a powerful group backed by the count of Champagne was working to establish an order of knights and have them housed in or near the Temple. Fouchet suspected that Count Hugh established Clairvaux Abbey specifically so that Bernard could be positioned as a champion of the Order within the Church.

A 19th-century depiction of the Chapter of the Order of Templars, held in Paris on April 22nd 1147. (The Bridgeman Art Library Ltd. / Alamy)

THE CRUSADES

From 1095 to 1272 European armies fought to recapture Jerusalem and other holy sites in the Middle East that had been taken from the Byzantine Empire during the expansion of Islam in the 7th century.

The First Crusade (1095–99) succeeded in recapturing Jerusalem. Four Christian states were established: the Kingdom of Jerusalem, the Country of Edessa, the Principality of Antioch, and the County of Tripoli.

The Second Crusade was launched in 1147 after Muslim forces recaptured the town of Edessa, but ended without any significant victories. For the next 40 years the future of the Crusader kingdoms hung in the balance.

Following Saladin's victory at the Battle of Hattin in 1187 the Crusader kingdoms collapsed: the Third and Fourth crusades failed to re-establish them. Four more crusades (or five, according to some historians) tried unsuccessfully to conquer Egypt.

Bernard of Clairvaux, who championed the founding of the Templars, was the nephew of one of the original nine knights and an intimate of the Count of Champagne. (Kohl-Illustration / Alamy)

The Order Grows

After the success of the Council of Troyes, Hugues de Payens returned to the Holy Land with a retinue of some 300 knights. During the next two decades, the Order grew rapidly.

The Templars acquired lands in the Holy Land and in almost every kingdom in Europe. Some were gifts but others were the properties of new members, who were required to hand over all of their possessions upon joining. Although individual Templars were sworn to poverty, the Order itself was under no such restriction.

In 1146 the Templars adopted the *cross pattée*, the splayed cross that became their most distinctive symbol. With the red cross on their white mantles – which only they, by papal decree, had the right to wear – they accompanied King Louis VII of France on the Second Crusade.

Despite the failure of the Second Crusade, the Templars continued to grow in reputation and influence. Their independence from kings placed them above national interests and gave them a trusted role in international diplomacy. In England, the Master of the Temple was often called to the king's Parliament, where he took precedence over all the priors and abbots in the land.

The Templars' growing wealth was put to good use. They lent money to most of Europe's rulers, and to some in the Muslim world. Their network of preceptories throughout Europe and the Middle East allowed them to set up a primitive banking system: travelers could deposit money at a Templar preceptory in their homeland, receiving in exchange a letter of credit which allowed them to draw cash at any Templar preceptory along their way.

The Order possessed its own ports, shipyards, and fleet. Its captains were among the first Europeans to navigate using the magnetic compass. It acquired a great deal of scientific knowledge – lost in Europe since the fall of Rome – from Middle Eastern sources.

The Order's growing power, it was said, made it arrogant. When Henry III of England tried to confiscate some of their domains, the English Master of the Order replied with a veiled threat: "So long as thou dost exercise justice, thou wilt reign. But if you infringe it, thou wilt cease to be king." This was an unthinkable thing to say to a European monarch. Even popes did not claim the power to make and unmake kings.

Templar initiation ceremony from c. 1280. (Artwork by Wayne Reynolds Osprey Publishing from WAR 91: *Knight Templar*)

According to some sources, the Templars made a practice of recruiting excommunicated knights. Forbidden access to divine salvation by the pope, these men were received by the Order and given absolution by its priests. To the Templars, the Church's most dreaded weapon was impotent.

To the Templars' alleged arrogance and disdain for the Church, some commentators added other vices. "To drink like a Templar" became a cliché of the times. Many looked askance upon their dealings with Muslim potentates and with the Assassins. In the dynastic squabble that followed the death of King Baldwin IV of Jerusalem in 1185, Grand Master Gerard de Ridefort betrayed an oath to the dead king and brought the Christian states in the Holy Land to the brink of civil war. Two years later, he urged the attack on Muslim forces at Hattin that resulted in the near annihilation of the Christian army.

As Muslim forces steadily reconquered the Crusader states, the Templars lived up to their reputation for discipline and heroism. But in 1291 Muslim forces captured Acre, the last Crusader outpost in the Holy Land. Grand Master Guillaume de Beaujeu fell in the final assault, which ended with the fortress collapsing on top of attackers and defenders alike.

The fall of Acre was a blow that resonated throughout the Christian world, and popular opinion turned even more against the Templars.

Outremer Lost

The Templars moved their headquarters to Cyprus, and then to Paris. There were some attempts to regain lost Crusader territories, including an anti-Muslim alliance with the Mongol Great Khan. The Templars maintained a garrison on the tiny island of Arwad just off the coast of Tripoli as a possible bridgehead for a renewed invasion, but this fell to the Egyptian Mamluks in 1302, taking with it any prospect of re-establishing the Crusader kingdoms.

The Knights Hospitaller, another knightly religious order, moved their headquarters to Rhodes after conquering the island in 1309, and established themselves as rulers there and on some neighboring islands. Meanwhile the Teutonic Knights had been expanding their *Ordensstaat* (Order-State) in the Baltic for almost 80 years. According to Fouchet, the Templars also wanted to establish a state of their own. Their initial objective was to take over the Kingdom of Jerusalem, but with the loss of the Holy Land they began to look elsewhere.

Toulouse

Toulouse was the major city in the Languedoc region of southern France. In the 14th century, the Languedoc had its own dialect, Occitan, and had closer ties to the Spanish kingdoms of Aragon and Catalonia than to Paris. It was only after the brutal Albigensian Crusade that the French kings cemented their hold on the region.

Many wealthy landowners suspected of Cathar leanings had donated land to the Templars. Bertrand de Blanchefort, the Order's fourth Grand Master, came from a Cathar family, and his descendants fought on the Cathar side during the Albigensian Crusade.

Despite their sworn allegiance to the pope, the Templars maintained a policy of neutrality during the Crusade. Contemporary accounts report that they hid Cathar refugees and sometimes took up arms in their defense. A large number of Cathars found safety by joining the Order.

The counts of Toulouse had been leading Cathars, and after the Albigensian Crusade their lands and domains became the property of the French crown.

Knight Templar in full armor c.1290. (Artwork by Wayne Reynolds Osprey Publishing from WAR 91: *Knight Templar*)

THE ASSASSINS

The Assassins, or *Hashashin*, were an offshoot of the Ismaili sect of Islam. They used murder, among many other methods, to achieve their ends. At the time of the Crusades they were virtually independent of Muslim rulers, answering only to their own leader, the Old Man of the Mountain.

The Assassins were not ardently opposed to the Crusaders. From time to time Christian leaders even employed their services as hired murderers, and they are known to have had some dealings with the Templars. Deeper and more sinister links have been hinted at down the centuries, but never proven.

The Cathars

The Cathars (also known as the Albigensians from their stronghold of Albi) were the last, and perhaps the largest, group to challenge Rome's domination of western Christianity. They believed that Jesus had been mortal rather than divine, and that personal virtue was the key to salvation. The popes, on the other hand, maintained that no one could be saved if they did not receive absolution from a Catholic priest.

The Holy Grail

Fouchet's documents had evidently remained hidden since the siege of Toulouse, and indicate very close links between the Cathars and the Templars. Certain documents made mention of the "Saint Graal" – the Holy Grail – which is linked to the Templars in many legends. The songs and poems of the troubadours, a group long associated with the Cathars, include some of the earliest known Grail legends.

Like almost everything to do with the Grail, these documents are cryptic, confusing, and contradictory. However, through careful reading and painstaking research Fouchet reached a startling conclusion: the Grail was real, and it was either in the Templars' keeping, or it was the Templars themselves. De Payens and his companions had found something beneath the Temple, and it had been in Toulouse briefly before the Albigensian Crusade.

The documents also indicate that the Holy Grail was the source of the Templars' great wealth and power, and that they felt a desperate need to keep it hidden from both kings and popes until the time was right to reveal its nature. Letters from Templar Grand Master Gilbert Horal to Count Raymond of Toulouse mention secret gifts of "false Grails" to churches in Italy and Spain, and discuss the count's sponsorship of various poets – including the celebrated Chrétien de Troyes – to help "safeguard the true Grail."

The implications of these letters are profound. Fouchet concluded that the Templars and the counts of Toulouse were part of a century-long conspiracy to promote a false Grail tradition in Europe, in order to divert attention from the "true Grail." But what was this "true Grail?"

The Holy Grail

The Templars have been associated with the Grail since the early troubadour tales of the late 12th century. In at least one version of the Grail Quest tale, Sir Galahad's shield bears a red cross on a white ground – definite Templar iconography – and for centuries painters have shown him wearing a white surcoat with a red cross.

Fouchet's work centers on the Holy Grail, and he arrives at a startling conclusion about its true nature. But first, it is necessary to summarize the various theories and stories about the Grail that have grown up over the last thousand years.

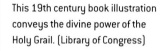

This 19th century book illustration conveys the divine power of the Holy Grail. (Library of Congress)

The Cup

In the troubadour tales and the Arthurian tradition that draws upon them, the Holy Grail is a cup or bowl that was closely associated with Jesus. According to most accounts it was the cup he used at the Last Supper, and some say that it was also used to catch some of his blood when he died on the cross.

In Arthurian tradition, the Holy Grail was brought to Britain by Joseph of Arimathea and hidden near Glastonbury. It miraculously appeared at King Arthur's court at Pentecost, the festival that commemorates the Last Supper. After the vision or manifestation had faded, almost all the knights of the Round Table vowed to find it, and so the Grail Quest began. In the end, only three knights – Galahad, Percival, and Bors – were sufficiently pure in spirit to complete the quest.

The troubadours took up the Arthurian tale and embellished it in their own tradition, extending and deepening its allegorical content. The symbolic meaning of the Holy Grail has been debated ever since.

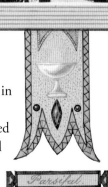

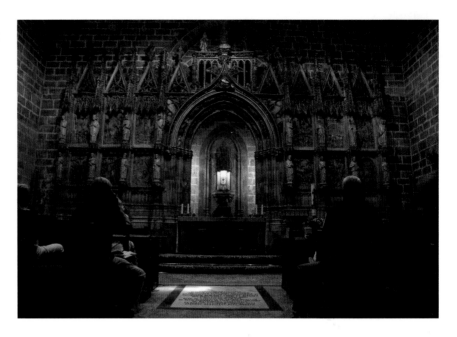

The Valencia Chalice is claimed by some to be the Holy Grail. (Miguel A. Muñoz Pellicer / Alamy)

The Holy Chalice

Catholic tradition maintains that the Holy Chalice with which Jesus conducted the first communion was brought to Rome by St Peter. It remained in the possession of the bishops of Rome until 258 when the pagan Roman government demanded that all Christian relics should be handed over to the state. Pope Sixtus II handed it over to St Lawrence, who had a Spanish soldier named Proselius take it to safety in Spain.

The Catholic Church is officially silent on the matter of the Holy Grail. Cups displayed in the cathedrals of Valencia, Spain and Genoa, Italy have both been linked to the Holy Chalice.

The Valencia chalice came to the cathedral from King Alfonso VII of Castile in 1200; the king used it as collateral for a loan that he never repaid. An inventory list, allegedly from the 3rd century, claims that the cup was one of the relics smuggled out of Rome by St Lawrence. The first reliable document describing the chalice dates from 1134. Several recent popes have used this cup to celebrate communion in Valencia Cathedral.

RELICS

In the Middle Ages, Catholic Europe was in the grip of a mania for collecting holy relics. A good relic could transform an unremarkable church into a highly profitable pilgrim destination. With the success of the First Crusade relics poured back to Europe.

The Holy Grail is among the most powerful Christian relics because of its association with the blood of Jesus. Even if one discounts the story that it was used to catch his blood at the crucifixion, its use at the Last Supper speaks to one of the most powerful mysteries of the Catholic Church: the moment when wine turns to redeeming blood at the climax of the Mass.

The Genoa chalice is mentioned by Guillaume de Tyre in 1170. Allegedly found in the mosque at Caesarea in 1101, it was thought to have been carved out of a huge emerald, and was given to the Genoese in payment of a debt. An alternative story from Spanish sources claims that it was looted from the Moors in the sack of Almeria in 1147. The cup was taken to Paris after Napoleon's conquest of Italy and returned broken, which revealed it to be made of green glass rather than emerald.

Fouchet found it significant that the first historical traces of both these cups appear in the 12th century. He suspected that they are early examples of the "false Grails" mentioned in the letters of Grand Master Gilbert Horal.

The Holy Blood

The documents of the "Plantard conspiracy" maintain that the term "Holy Grail" arises from a misreading of some ancient text. Instead of the French "Saint Graal," one should read "Sang Réal," or "Royal Blood."

Thus, the Grail becomes the holy bloodline of Jesus, whose children by Mary Magdalene were the ancestors of France's Merovingian kings. Some Grail romances speak of a "Grail Castle" and a "Grail Family" guarded by an order of knights who bear a distinct resemblance to the Templars. Plantard and his successors take this to mean that the bloodline of Jesus is still in existence, kept safe by the Templars (or by a related organization named the Priory of Sion) until the time is right to make its existence known.

Fouchet dismisses the Plantard story out of hand, likening it to the "false Grails" of Gilbert Horal's letters. He believed it was concocted shortly after World War II after the discovery of the Dead Sea Scrolls and Nag Hammadi manuscripts and promulgated in English via the book *The Holy Blood and the Holy Grail*. According to Fouchet, the Templars feared the imminent exposure of the "true Grail." By creating an elaborate false trail leading to the alleged descendants of Jesus, the Plantard conspirators hoped to sow confusion and, in Fouchet's words, "render the whole matter so ridiculous as to make serious academic enquiry impossible."

Metaphors

Scholars have long suspected that the Holy Grail of the troubadour romances is a metaphor rather than a physical object. It has been argued that the metaphor has a number of layers, with meanings that differ according to one's level of initiation into the mysteries.

Salvation

The simplest interpretation of the Grail Quest is that it is a search for salvation; the Grail reveals itself only to the pure in heart. Even Lancelot, the greatest of Arthur's knights, fails in the quest because he has a single sin on his conscience; the guilt of his romantic attachment to Guinevere. The name

In keeping with the Templar legend of the nine poor knights, the Order's seal showed two Templars sharing a single horse. (PD-US)

of the Grail Castle, given by Wulfram von Eschenbach as Munsalvaesche, has been interpreted as *Mons Salvationis*, or "Mount of Salvation."

If they are no more than allegories of the quest for spiritual salvation, then the Catholic Church could hardly object to the Grail romances. However, reading between the lines it can be seen that the Grail Quest is a search for salvation through personal endeavor rather than by the Catholic sacrament of absolution. Fouchet notes that both the Cathars and the Templars were accused of denying absolution and the other sacraments of the Catholic Church.

Secret Teachings

Some scholars believe that the Holy Grail was a symbol for the teachings of Jesus, brought to Europe by those who knew him personally: people like Joseph of Arimathea and Mary Magdalene. If the blood, or essence, of Jesus was in his teachings, then the Grail was anything or anyone from whom these teachings could be consumed.

Within the last hundred years, the Dead Sea Scrolls and the Nag Hammadi manuscripts have shed considerable light on early Christian thinking. By the Middle Ages, almost a thousand years of Church councils had decided what religious works were "canon" – to be included in the Bible – and what were apocryphal. Several books, including gospels, were amended to make them more acceptable to the Church. Reading or preaching from works outside the approved canon was heresy, so the apocryphal traditions could only be kept alive secretly, under the cover of codes and symbols.

Given the established connection between the Cathars and the troubadours, the Holy Grail makes an excellent symbol for a Cathar religion that went underground after the massacres of the Albigensian Crusade.

The Quest for the Holy Grail, then, could be seen as an allegory for a process of mystical initiation, whereby the initiates were prepared mentally and spiritually for deeper levels of knowledge. The accounts of Templar rituals that emerged under torture suggest that the Order practiced some process of mystical initiation. It is certain that the Assassins did so, and so do the Freemasons, the Rosicrucians, the Illuminati, and other groups that claim Templar ancestry.

In the context of an underground religion, initiation would provide some protection against Church persecution. The greatest knowledge was only made available to those who had proved they could be trusted, and had prepared their minds to accept what was about to be revealed to them.

Fouchet supported the idea that the Holy Grail was used as a symbol for secret Cathar and Templar religious teachings, but he believes that it could also have a deeper meaning. To those who had reached the highest levels of Cathar initiation and the highest ranks of the Templar hierarchy, the Holy Grail also included the secrets that Hugues de Payens had found beneath the Temple of Solomon.

Solomon's Stables. The underground chamber is now part of the al-Aqsa Mosque. (PD-US)

ALCHEMY

Accounts of the Templars' trials (see next chapter) frequently referred to the worship of a bearded head. In the coded language of alchemy, the phrase *Caput Mortuum*, or "Dead Head," referred to the *nigredo* or "blackening" that was said to take place in the final stages of the creation of the Philosopher's Stone. It has been suggested that the accusations of idolatry may be garbled and partly understood reports of alchemical experiments.

Fouchet was convinced that the Templars did amass considerable alchemical knowledge. However, he dismisses the idea that the worship of a head was a coded reference to alchemy. Instead, he was convinced that the bearded head in Templar rituals represented John the Baptist. Despite this, Fouchet did believe that the Templars mastered the secrets of alchemy. No known alchemical texts have been firmly linked to the Templars, and most historians believe that the Order's great wealth came exclusively from their widespread land holdings and banking operations. However, Fouchet argues that even these sources would have been exhausted quickly given the level of Templar spending. The Order regularly made enormous loans to many European monarchs, built huge and expensive castles, and maintained a large mercenary force to man their bases and supplement their members on the battlefield.

King Solomon was reputed to be a powerful magician as well as a wise ruler. (PD-US)

The Treasure of Solomon

There have been rumors of a hidden treasure beneath Solomon's Temple for centuries. In addition to gold and silver, the lost treasures were said to include the Ark of the Covenant and the magical library of Solomon. In Jewish and Islamic lore, the king was a powerful sorcerer as well as a wise ruler.

According to Fouchet, the "true Grail" consisted of treasures – mystical as well as material – that de Payens and his companions recovered from beneath the Temple between 1119 and 1127. Over time, the term also came to stand for an ideal state that the Templars intended to establish in Jerusalem, and which they have attempted to create several times in Europe and North America. Fouchet's research is too extensive to reproduce here in detail, but the key points are as follows.

The Troyes Cabal and the Counts of Champagne

According to Fouchet, the "Troyes cabal" acquired documents that pointed to the location of certain hidden treasures. Count Hugh of Champagne visited Jerusalem to assess the situation, and upon returning he put an elaborate plan into motion. He established Bernard as the abbot of Clairvaux, to give himself a powerful ally inside the Church, and instructed de Payens, de Montbard, and their companions to win King Baldwin's confidence and gain access to the Temple Mount.

The plan took more than nine years to complete. The last of the treasure was found and removed by 1127, and no one outside of the "Troyes cabal" was any the wiser. Bernard of Clairvaux used his position within the Church to help found the Order of the Knights Templar, and the Order acquired property in Jerusalem to house the treasure.

The counts of Champagne, who played a role in the founding of the Order, continue to figure in the story. Most of them made at least one trip to the Middle East.

Hugh's great-grand-nephew Henry II of Champagne became king of Jerusalem in 1192, but he came to the title by marriage and it passed from the family upon his death. Henry's brother Theobald III married into the royal house of Navarre, and his son Thibault IV, known as Thibault the Troubadour, became king of Navarre as well as count of Champagne.

Theobald's two sons, Theobald V and Henry III, were both unable to produce a male heir. Henry's daughter Joan succeeded him but constant plots led her and her mother to flee to the French court when Joan was just ten years old. She married Philip le Bel, and as a result he became count of Champagne as well as king of Navarre. It is interesting to speculate whether he found something in the court papers of Champagne which piqued his interest in the Templars. When Joan died in childbirth in 1304, at least one chronicler suspected her husband of being responsible for her death.

Solomon's Library

Large caches of documents were found along with the gold and silver. De Payens learned the ancient languages needed to study these manuscripts and found, to his great surprise, that he had the magical library of Solomon in his hands.

Mystical diagram of Solomon's Temple, as prophesied by Ezekiel and planned in the building scheme of the Knights Templar

A mystical diagram of Solomon's Temple, incorporating the shape of the Templar Cross. (Bridgeman Art Library)

After they received papal approval the Templars became wealthy and powerful. No doubt some of their wealth came from their shipping and banking businesses, but their whole operation was underpinned by the Temple treasure, both the gold and silver they recovered, and the techniques of alchemy that de Payens had extracted from Solomon's scrolls.

(OVERLEAF) A classic depiction of the Knights Templar as guardians of the sacred cup. Fouchet believed that the image of the Holy Grail was a symbol for a deeper secret.

The Templar State

As de Payens read more of Solomon's library, he conceived the plan of establishing a new Jerusalem, not in its current form as a European-style feudal state, but as it had been in Solomon's time. The Templar Grand Masters, wielding Solomon's wisdom and magical power, would rule as priest-kings. Being celibate and owing their office to election rather than inheritance, the Templar state would be immune to the dynastic squabbles that plagued Europe and the Crusader states.

The Templar Creed

Inspired by the writings he studied and the religious ideas he found in the Holy Land, Hugues de Payens developed a Templar creed that fused Judaism, Christianity, and Islam along Cathar lines. Claiming descent from Solomon and bolstered by eyewitness accounts of Jesus' life that the Church had suppressed, this Templar religion could unite all the peoples of Europe and Asia and bring lasting peace to the Middle East.

De Payens knew that the Templar creed could not coexist with the Church of Rome, since the pope claimed supreme power in all religious matters. For the time being, the Templar Creed had to be kept secret, restricted to those who had passed the highest degree of initiation. The vast majority of Templars knew only that they were in a military order under a monastic rule, and that their commanders possessed some secret knowledge to which they themselves might aspire.

Hattin

The plan all but collapsed in the aftermath of the Battle of Hattin in 1187. The Templar Grand Master, Gerard de Ridefort, was overconfident and pushed for an attack; however the Crusader forces found themselves surrounded and hampered by choking smoke. Unable to see and hardly able to breathe, the Crusaders broke up into small, disoriented groups that were easy for Saladin's forces to overcome.

As soon as the news of Hattin broke, the Templars in Jerusalem moved the treasure to Acre. Left almost defenseless, Jerusalem fell. After the Third and Fourth crusades failed to retake the city, the Templars accepted that they might have to create their Jerusalem elsewhere and began work on a contingency plan.

The Cathars and the Troubadours

De Ridefort's successor as Grand Master, Robert de Sablé, purchased Cyprus from Richard I of England, but quickly realized that the island was ungovernable. He charged his successor, Gilbert Horal, with preparing the ground in the Cathar south of France. Horal made contact with Cathar leaders and found their beliefs to be very compatible with the Templar creed as formulated by Hugues de Payens.

Horal also developed the growing troubadour tradition, where the Holy Grail had just begun to emerge as an allegorical symbol for religious truth. By establishing the image of Templar-like knights as the guardians of the Grail, he hoped to smooth the way toward the establishment of a Templar state in the Cathar lands.

Within the Order's highest ranks, the Holy Grail became a symbol and a codeword, both for the treasure of Solomon and for the whole Templar enterprise. A series of Grail hoaxes was concocted to cover the Order's tracks. Ornate cups of a suitable age were discreetly distributed to several churches and cathedrals, and poets across Europe were encouraged to create more imaginative and contradictory Grail romances.

Initially the project progressed well, but the growth of the Cathar movement caused alarm in both Paris and the Vatican. By 1229 the Albigensian Crusade had all but destroyed the Cathars and the kings of France ruled in place of the counts of Toulouse. Although the Order was able to give refuge to large numbers of fugitive Cathars, the eyes of the king and the pope were watching the south too closely for any Templar plan to advance there.

Acre

The Templars fought to maintain their foothold in the east, but over the next century the Crusader kingdoms were steadily overcome. By 1291 only Acre remained, and it fell in a desperate siege.

Just as the Albigensian Crusade had thwarted Templar ambitions in Provence, the loss of Acre ended their hopes of regaining Jerusalem. The Templars were in disarray after the losses of the siege, and Beaujeu's successor Thibaud Gaudin died the following year, leaving Jacques de Molay with the task of rebuilding the Order.

Downfall

Philip le Bel

Like most European kings of his time, Phillippe IV of France (known as Philip "le Bel", or "handsome") was in constant and desperate need of money. When

he ascended the throne of France in 1285 he inherited the debts of his father's war with Aragon. In 1293 he tried to trick Edward I of England into relinquishing Aquitaine, but this only led to another expensive war with England and its Flemish allies.

Matters reached a crisis in 1306. Philip turned first to the Jews, expelling them from France and seizing their property in an act known as the Great Exile. He then called in all the loans they had made to his Christian subjects. When this measure did not refill his coffers sufficiently, Philip repeated the exercise with the Lombard bankers in France. In addition, he debased the coinage so recklessly that his coins lost two-thirds of their face value.

The resulting financial crisis led to rioting, and Philip was forced to take refuge from the mob in the Paris Temple. It was there that he saw the great wealth of the Knights Templar. But Philip could not attack the Templars without first securing the co-operation of the pope.

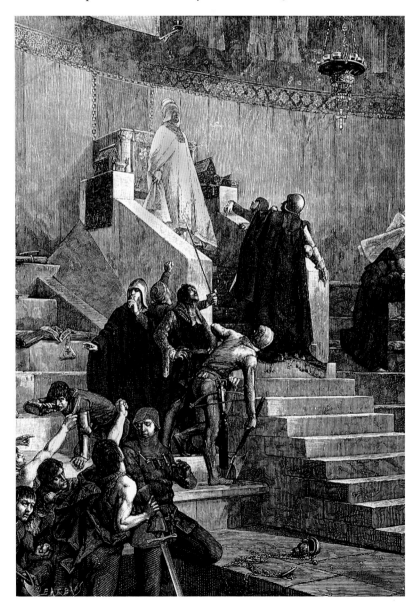

The Problem of the Pope

Philip's relations with the papacy were less than cordial. After levying taxes on the previously inviolate abbots and clergy, Philip had made an enemy of Pope Boniface VIII. By 1303, Philip had denounced the pope before the French clergy as a criminal heretic and Boniface had excommunicated him.

Later that year an army led by members of the powerful Italian Colonna family – and accompanied by Philip's chief minister Guillaume de Nogaret – surprised Boniface at his retreat at Agnani outside Rome. Despite being threatened and badly beaten, Boniface refused to resign. He died within a month, allegedly of kidney-stones.

Boniface was succeeded by Benedict XI, who lifted Philip's excommunication but excommunicated Nogaret and all the Italians who had attacked Boniface at Agnani. Benedict died suddenly before completing a year in office. Nogaret was suspected of poisoning him, but no proof was ever found.

Philip decided to make his own pope, Raymond de Goth, the archbishop of Bordeaux. His election was no easy matter; he was an archbishop, not a cardinal, and he was French rather than Italian. The conclave was deadlocked for almost a year before he was elected on June 5, 1305, becoming Pope Clement V.

Rome was lawless and full of anti-French sentiment at the time, so Clement established his court at Poitiers. The count of Poitiers was the king's second son and eventual successor, Philip the Tall. Perhaps Clement felt he needed the protection of the French royal house, or perhaps Philip decided to keep his new pope on a short leash. Clement undid all of Boniface's measures and seemed ready to oblige Philip in every way.

Fouchet notes two details that many historians fail to mention. First, before taking the throne of France, Philip had become count of Champagne through his marriage to Joan of Navarre. Second, his minister Nogaret was the son of a condemned Cathar from Toulouse.

The Templars, a count of Champagne, and the son of a Cathar, could this be mere coincidence? Fouchet thought not. He believed that Philip – or more likely, the brilliant schemer Nogaret – found something in the ducal papers of Champagne that shed light on the "Troyes cabal" and the Templar secret of the "true Grail."

The Templar fortress in Paris became the Order's headquarters after the fall of Acre in 1291. (TPM Photostock / Alamy)

Fouchet was convinced that lust for the Templars' fabled wealth was not Philip's only motivation to take action against the Order, but he was unable to find any evidence for his theory. Before his fatal visit to Troyes, Fouchet spent several fruitless weeks in the National Archives in Paris. His notes reflect a growing conviction that key documents from the reign of Philip le Bel had been hidden or tampered with.

Preparations

With a co-operative pope, Philip found an excuse to attack the Templars in the accusations of one Squin de Flexian, who had been expelled from the Order for heresy and other offenses.

Flexian was imprisoned with a Florentine named Noffo Dei – who by some accounts was also a former Templar – and the two bargained for their freedom by offering to testify against the Order. To add further weight to their accusations, it was stated that Cardinal Cantilupo, Pope Clement's chamberlain, had been an associate of the Templars since the age of 11, and had confessed some of their doings to his master.

A later image of Jacques de Molay. (Mary Evans Picture Library / Alamy)

Shortly after he became Pope, Clement invited the Grand Masters of the Templars and the Hospitallers to a meeting. Its stated purpose was to discuss possible measures against the expanding Ottoman Empire, but the Templars and the Hospitallers had a long-standing rivalry which Clement longed to resolve. As the theoretical head of these two formidable fighting forces he could only profit from their unity – perhaps even becoming strong enough to throw off Philip's domination.

The Hospitaller Grand Master Guillaume de Villaret was occupied fighting the Saracens in Rhodes, but his Templar counterpart Jacques de Molay sailed for France.

De Molay reached Paris in early 1307. Philip received him cordially, making him godfather to one of his sons and inviting him to act as a pall-bearer at the state funeral of the king's sister-in-law. In Poitiers, de Molay and Clement discussed a possible new crusade and de Molay stated his opposition to Clement's plan to merge the Templars and the Hospitallers into a single order.

Clouds Gather

Returning to Paris, de Molay heard that rumors were circulating about the Templars and their activities. He went back to Poitiers in about April with the preceptors of Outremer, Aquitaine, and France. After discussing the charges that had surfaced against the Order with the pope, it is said that de Molay and his companions returned to Paris in good heart.

Friday the 13th

At dawn on Friday, October 13, 1307, the king's seneschals throughout France opened sealed orders commanding them to arrest all Templars in their jurisdiction and take control of Templar properties and goods. The operation was carried out with startling speed and efficiency.

Fouchet particularly impressed that there is no record of any Templars anywhere in France resisting the king's officers. The Order could probably have mustered an army strong enough to make the king think twice, but they surrendered as peacefully as if they had been ordered to do so.

The Treasure

Fouchet suggests that Philip did not achieve the total surprise he needed. Although Clement had apparently tried to reassure him, de Molay was not so naive as to think the Order was safe. De Molay could not prevent the arrest of hundreds of Templars and the seizure of considerable property, but he did what he could to protect the Templars and their secret. Books were recalled and destroyed, and a letter to all French preceptories stressed that no outsiders should be given any information about Templar customs and rituals.

The Order's treasurer, Hugues de Peraud, and the preceptor of France, Gerard de Villers, were not captured until a few days after the raids. The deposition of one Jean de Chalons states that he saw de Villers and 50 horsemen leave the Temple accompanying three carts that carried chests hidden under straw. Other reports state that "a great treasure" was moved by road to the Order's naval base at La Rochelle, and loaded on to 18 galleys that sailed off and were never heard of again.

Fouchet believed that the "true Grail" was among the treasure smuggled out of Paris and loaded aboard the lost Templar fleet. Although there is no detailed report of what Clement said to de Molay and his preceptors, Fouchet thought it possible that the pope tried to bargain with the Templars, offering protection in exchange for the secret treasure.

If so, he failed. The "true Grail" was moved out of his reach, the Templars were arrested, and in the years that followed Clement was barely able to protect himself from the king.

A 19th-century print showing the interrogation of Jacques de Molay. (PD-US)

Examination and Trial

The examination of the captured Templars began within two days of the arrests. Some died under torture without admitting any wrongdoing. Others gave confessions that they later recanted, even though doing so meant death at the stake.

The Charges

The initial interrogations were based on the charges that had been made against the Order by Squin de Flexian. As torture wrung stranger and stranger confessions from the captured Templars, the investigation broadened.

Fouchet makes some interesting observations about the charges.

1. *Upon joining the Order, each Templar swore never to leave the order, and to further its interests by right or wrong.*

   The last part of this charge could be taken by the Order's enemies as proof of criminal intent, or at least of disregard for the law. Alternatively, it could be a malicious interpretation of an oath to further the Order's interests by any means in their power. In any case, Pope Innocent's bull of 1139 had specifically placed the Order above the laws of the countries in which it operated.

2. *The heads of the Order are in a secret alliance with the Saracens and are sympathetic to Islam. They make every novice spit and trample upon the Cross, and commit other blasphemies.*

   This is the main charge of heresy against the Templars. It is examined in more detail in a later chapter.

3. *Novices who try to leave the Order are secretly killed. The Templars resort to*

abortion and infanticide when women become pregnant by them.

The second part of this charge was also leveled against priests and abbots at various times throughout the Middle Ages and the Reformation. Like the Templars, they were required to be celibate, and any accidental pregnancies had to be covered up.

4. *They pretend to be good Christians but secretly deny the authority of the Church and the pope; they scorn the sacraments, especially confession and penance.*

   Similar charges had been made against the Cathars during the Albigensian Crusade.

5. *Leading Templars are guilty of excessive debauchery, and imprison members who express repugnance at their excesses.*

   This is a fairly standard subsidiary charge against heretics of all kinds, going back at least to the Bogomil heresy of the 10th century. It has been claimed that the English word "bugger" originated as a corruption either of "Bogomil" or of "Bulgar," from the Bogomils' original homeland.

6. *Their preceptories are sinks of every imaginable crime and vice.*

   This vague statement merely reiterates parts of other charges.

7. *The Order favors the Saracens and works to place them in control of the Holy Land.*

   The Holy Land was already in Muslim hands when these charges were made, and the Templars had been among its most determined defenders.

ISLAMIC SCIENCE

Mystical knowledge aside, it is certain that the Templars went further than many of their contemporaries in embracing the wealth of scientific and other knowledge they found in the Muslim world – knowledge that the Church regarded both as a threat to its self-proclaimed monopoly on education and as suspect on account of its infidel source.

At the time of the Crusades, the Islamic world was far in advance of Christendom in the arts and sciences. To take one example, the concept of the number zero came from the Muslim world, and the Arabic system of numerals replaced the Roman system in Europe and remains in use today. Following Arthur C. Clarke's maxim that any sufficiently advanced technology is indistinguishable from magic, many in Europe regarded the Islamic world – and the knowledge that came from it – as dangerous and possibly diabolical.

It has been suggested that the Templars – or "free masons" under Templar protection – brought back advanced ideas about architecture that resulted in the development of the Gothic style of Europe's great cathedrals. The Order's infirmaries employed standards of cleanliness and hygiene that were very advanced for the day, and its surgeons demonstrated knowledge of medicines and drugs – including a tantalizing reference to mold, which makes one wonder if they had stumbled upon penicillin or something similar. More controversially, they regarded epilepsy as a treatable physical condition rather than a sign of demonic possession.

In his notes, Fouchet compares the Templars' openness to Islamic and Jewish science to the social and religious revolution that accompanied the European Enlightenment three centuries after the Order's downfall. In his opinion, the Templar State (see p.22) was modeled on the ideals of enlightened despotism that would later form a major strand of Enlightenment thinking.

However, charges of pro-Muslim leanings continued to be made alongside charges of heresy.

8. *The Master of the Order is installed in secret, and it is suspected that he repudiates Christianity as part of the ceremony.*

Outsiders were barred from attending most Templar ceremonies, giving rise to all kinds of speculations about what these ceremonies involved.

9. *Many of the Order's rules are unlawful and contrary to Christianity. Therefore the members are forbidden to reveal them to anyone, on pain of lifelong imprisonment.*

Again, the Templars' secrecy is equated with having something to hide. If Philip knew what the secret was, he must have had a good reason to want it kept from the public record.

10. *No vice or crime committed for the good of the Order is held to be a sin.*

This is simply a reiteration of the first charge.

A 14th-century image of Templars being burned, from the British National Library. (PD-US)

Fouchet summarizes the charges against the Templars under five headings:

- They ignored the laws of the land and the laws of the Church when these were contrary to the Order's interests.
- They flouted the authority of the Church and may have rejected Christianity entirely.
- They were secret Muslim sympathizers.
- They operated in secret and took drastic action against any members who threatened to break that secrecy.
- They were prone to all kinds of moral vices and excesses.

Fouchet found it significant that the initial charges do not include any of witchcraft. Henry Cornelius Agrippa discussed the Templars in his *De Occulta Philosophia* of 1531, hinting that black magic formed a part of the Templar heresy, and since then the legend of Templar magic has grown considerably. To Fouchet, this omission suggested that the king knew something of the "true Grail" and did not want this knowledge to leak out.

The Interrogations

As the interrogation and torture continued, further details were added to the initial charges and new charges emerged. There were lurid accounts of obscene practices and homosexuality, just as there were – and would continue to be – in other cases involving heresy, witchcraft, and interrogation by torture.

Some Templars admitted to trampling and spitting upon the cross and worshiping a human head called Baphomet. Their interrogators questioned other Templars about Baphomet with varying results. Some agreed that it was a human head, but others said it took the form of a cat, or of a statue

Accusations that Templars spat and trampled upon the cross may be based on a misunderstanding of the Templar creed. (Mary Evans Picture Library / Alamy)

of demonic aspect. The Church authorities concluded that Baphomet, being clearly a demon, could take many forms. As to the name, it was generally agreed to be a corruption of Mahomet, strengthening the charge of Muslim sympathies.

Clement and Avignon

Pope Clement apparently became uneasy as the interrogations proceeded. Philip wrote him a sharp letter reminding him that this was God's work and he, the king, would answer to God alone. Clement responded by demanding that the inquisitions of each bishop should be confirmed by a provincial council, and that Clement himself would interrogate the Order's masters personally.

This measure resulted in a spate of confessions and retractions, alongside allegations that the heads of the Order had confessed freely and spontaneously to Clement himself. At this point, for reasons that remain unclear, Clement decided to quit Poitiers. He headed for Bordeaux, but was stopped by the king's forces and forced to return.

However, Clement was not finished trying to thwart the king. In August of 1308 he issued what amounted to a blanket pardon for all charges of heresy that had been leveled against the Templars.

Barely six months later he left Poitiers again, this time for Avignon, an independent papal territory where the king of France could not touch him. He spent the rest of his reign there.

In 1311 Clement summoned the Council of Vienne, which formally refused to convict the Templars of heresy. Even so, Clement officially abolished the Order in March 1312. Templar lands and estates in France were granted to the Hospitallers, although the king continued to hold them; he also appropriated all the assets of Templar banking operations in France.

Fouchet was intrigued by Clement's maneuverings during this period. If he warned de Molay about Philip's plan, perhaps he hoped to save the Templars. If they all died, the "true Grail" would be lost to him, but if he saved them he might yet lay his hands on it and gain the military strength he needed to stand up to the king of France.

Most significant to Fouchet was Clement's demand that he alone would interrogate the Order's masters. Clement seems to have realized that only they knew the secret of the "true Grail," and this was information that he desperately wanted to keep out of the king's hands.

When events spiraled out of his control, Clement apparently tried to flee France. He pardoned the Templars for heresy, which was the most convincing of the charges against them. Although this pardon was somehow lost or suppressed for almost 700 years, the Council of Vienne stated clearly that the Templars were not heretics.

Was Clement paving the way for some scheme to rehabilitate the Templars? Although he had not been able to prevent the arrests and interrogations, perhaps he still hoped to save them. At this point in his narrative, Fouchet introduces some facts about Raymond de Goth that shed an interesting light on his actions as Pope Clement V. While admitting that the evidence is all circumstantial, Fouchet believed that Clement knew about Templar–Cathar links, and may have known the truth about the "true Grail."

Raymond had spent much of his ecclesiastical career in Cathar country. He had been the bishop of Saint-Bertrand-des-Comminges, and greatly enlarged its cathedral. The town is of Roman origin. Herod Antipas – the New Testament's King Herod – was exiled to Lugdunum Convenarum, as it was called then, by the Emperor Caligula. Based on the Toulouse documents, Fouchet thought that some document from Herod's exile – perhaps found during Clement's improvements – touched upon the Temple and the treasure the Templars had found there.

By the time Clement was safe in Avignon, though, it seems that the king had already done too much damage. Clement was able to quash the heresy charges, and his actions had bought enough time for the Order's secrets, and many of its key surviving members, to win their way to safety. By officially dissolving the Order in 1312, he drew a veil of secrecy over what was to follow. His death in 1314 thwarted whatever further plans he may have made.

Outside France

The monarchs of other European countries proved less amenable to Philip's demands for the extermination of all Templars.

His son-in-law Edward II of England banned the Order after some pressure, but allowed most English Templars to join other orders after light penances. Scotland was excommunicated at the time, and Clement's bull dissolving the Templars was never promulgated there. The duke of Lorraine, which was independent of France, exonerated the Templars, and their local preceptor advised them to shave their distinctive beards and melt into the local population.

The Templars of the German states threatened to take up arms against France and the pope. Their judges, perhaps intimidated, found them innocent of all charges. After the Order was dissolved, most Templars joined the Hospitallers or the Teutonic Knights. In Portugal the Templars simply changed their name to the Knights of Christ.

A Templar cross on the floor of a chapel in Portugal, where the Order changed its name to the Knights of Christ. (John Ferro Sims / Alamy)

De Molay's Curse

Jacques de Molay was sentenced to life imprisonment. When he and another senior Templar were paraded in public to have their sentence announced, they continued to protest their innocence. This so enraged Philip that he had de Molay burned at the stake on March 18, 1314 along with Geoffroi de Charney, the preceptor of Normandy.

It is claimed that Jacques de Molay spoke to Philip from the stake, summoning both the king and Pope Clement to meet him before God's throne of judgment. The official record states that his last words were "God knows who is wrong and who has sinned. Soon a calamity will take those who have condemned us to death." Clement and Philip both died within the year, and just 14 years after de Molay's execution the male line of Philip's Capetian dynasty had completely died out.

There has been much speculation about a "Templar curse" that destroyed Philip's line, but Fouchet regarded simple murder carried out by Templar agents as more probable.

The Accursed Pope

Clement died of sudden dysentery just 33 days after de Molay. The church where his body lay in state was struck by lightning, starting a fire that destroyed his body.

While dysentery was not uncommon in the 14th century, the suddenness and speed of Clement's death – and the timing – are provocative. Fouchet's notes indicate that he thought Clement was poisoned.

He explained the lightning strike by pointing out that medieval churches were usually taller than any surrounding building, making them more prone to lightning than their neighbors. The fire may have been set deliberately under cover of the storm, or it may have been entirely coincidental.

THE CHINON PARCHMENT

In 2001 a parchment was discovered in the Vatican archives. It had apparently been misfiled in 1628. Dated August 17–20, 1308, the parchment bore the names of several cardinals who had interrogated Jacques de Molay and other high-ranking Templars on behalf of Pope Clement.

As well as recording the testimony of these Templars, the parchment apparently absolves them of heresy. Possibly this document was Clement's attempt to rescue the Order from Philip's persecution, but it seems that the king was not to be denied.

The Last Capets

Philip le Bel died eight months after de Molay's execution, having suffered an accident – or according to some accounts, a stroke or seizure – while hunting. He was 29 years old and had been in good health all his life.

Philip's successor Louis X drank a quantity of cooled wine after a vigorous tennis game and died shortly after – from pleurisy or pneumonia, it is said, although poison was also suspected. His son John I, born five months later, lived for only five days.

Louis' brother Philip V reigned for five years but died of "multiple illnesses" after his rule was destabilized by popular hysteria following a rumor that foreign Muslims had employed French Jews to use lepers to poison the wells of major French cities. His only son, also called Philip, died in infancy.

Charles IV, the youngest son of Philip le Bel, reigned for another six years but also left no male heir. The French throne passed to the House of Valois, a minor branch of the Capet family, but a claim from Edward III of England led to the Hundred Years' War. This conflict actually lasted for 116 years, almost bankrupting both kingdoms and achieving no lasting result.

The Templar Creed

Fouchet believed that many of the heresy and witchcraft charges leveled against the Templars can be explained by the existence of what he calls a "Templar Creed" which blended Catharism with Gnostic and Johannite thinking and dismissed many of the core teachings of the Catholic Church. Inspired by religious texts brought back from the Holy Land, the Templar Creed also incorporated mystical ideas from Jewish and Islamic tradition that the Templars encountered during their time there.

It was the Templars' intention, Fouchet claimed, to bridge the divides between Christianity, Judaism, and Islam and create a new kingdom of Jerusalem ruled by philosopher-kings in the mold of Solomon himself. In the eyes of the Church, this made them the most dangerous kind of heretics.

Pope Clement abruptly dropped all charges of heresy against the Order. Based on the collected testimony – including some that was not given under torture – heresy is about the only one of the charges that could have been proved, which struck Fouchet as curious.

He speculated that the pope dropped the charges precisely because they *were* true. To go forward with trials against senior Templars would have brought information about the Templar Creed into the open. Fouchet believed that Clement quashed all further investigations into the heresy charges in order to cover up its existence.

According to Fouchet, Clement feared that the Catholic Church would be unable to compete against such a rational and well-reasoned heresy. Having destroyed the Cathars, the Church of Rome desperately needed to consolidate its hold on European religion. By drawing attention to the Templar Creed by proceeding with heresy trials, Clement might have unwillingly created a powerful competitor for the Catholic Church. Backed by the prestige of the Templars, such a religion would have been very attractive to any king or lord who had a political or financial dispute with a local bishop or abbot and wanted to assert his independence from Rome.

A fragment of the Gospel of Thomas from the Nag Hammadi library. In the Middle East the Templars encountered a great deal of religious thought that had been suppressed in Catholic Europe. (www.BibleLandPictures. com / Alamy)

Heresy

According to the common image of the Middle Ages, to be from western Europe was to be Roman Catholic – or to be burned for heresy. But the Church of Rome was simply the most aggressive of several Christian sects in Europe at the time, some of which commanded almost as many followers. It was not until the destruction of the Cathars in the 13th century that the papacy could begin to feel secure in its religious domination of Europe.

Witchcraft and heresy were inseparable in the medieval mind. Therefore if the Templars were indeed heretics, it was natural that they should also practice witchcraft.

The severed head worshiped by the Templars may be a symbol of John the Baptist. Painting by Caravaggio (PD-US)

The East

The Middle East of the 12th century was a hotbed of beliefs that the Catholic Church regarded as heretical. The Orthodox Church, based in Byzantium (now Istanbul), was the largest and held sway over most native Christian communities. In addition there were Gnostics, Manicheans, Mandaeans, and other groups – some with magical as well as theological traditions – and multiple Jewish and Muslim sects. Most of these groups had their own mystical traditions, and many historians believe that the alleged Templar heresy was at least partly influenced by the Order's encounters with groups such as these.

The Cathars

Several of the charges made against the Templars in 1307 had also been made against the Cathars a century earlier.

Several prominent Templars – including Bertrand de Blanchefort, the Order's fourth Grand Master – came from former Cathar families, and Fouchet believed that some brand of Catharism survived within the Order, concealed by the notorious secrecy of its rituals.

The Order's policy of neutrality during the Albigensian Crusade must also have given the Church cause for concern. It was unusual, to say the least, for a dedicated crusading order to take no part in an officially sanctioned crusade, and there were rumors that the Templars had secretly rendered assistance and safe passage to fugitive Cathars.

The Troubadours

The troubadours are generally regarded today as simple wandering minstrels, but in the years that followed the Albigensian Crusade they were far more than that. They were, it can be argued, a traveling propaganda machine keeping Cathar doctrine alive through complex allegories in their tales. They were also responsible for developing and spreading the Grail romances across Western Europe.

Many early troubadours were noblemen and wore the title "troubadour" proudly, composing songs and poems that mixed neo-Platonic and Cathar philosophy, Grail romances, satire against the Church of Rome, and themes from classical literature.

Here Fouchet found yet more links to Troyes and the court of Champagne. Chrétien de Troyes was a leading author of Grail romances, and as his name suggests he was born and raised in the capital of Champagne. Count Theobald IV, who ruled Champagne at the time of the Albigensian Crusade, was nicknamed "the Troubadour" and a number of his works have survived. He also went to the Holy Land and negotiated a treaty that returned the city of Jerusalem – along with Bethlehem, Nazareth, and other territories – to the kings of Jerusalem.

Fouchet's notes indicate that he thought of the troubadours as one arm of a secret society dedicated to keeping Cathar traditions alive and restoring the Crusader kingdom of Jerusalem. He believed that Count Theobald's main involvement was in the second mission, and that he merely dabbled in troubadour poetry. More is said about the kingdom of Jerusalem in a later chapter.

THE HERESIES

The most relevant heresies to the case of the Templars are described here briefly. Naturally, the entire teachings of each group were a good deal more complex.

GNOSTICISM: One of the earliest forms of Christianity, Gnosticism maintained that the individual could come to be one with God through a spiritual experience, without the need for churches and priests as intermediaries. This invalidated the sacraments of communion and absolution which the Church of Rome regarded as its most powerful mysteries.

MANDAEISM: This Mesopotamian sect, also known as the Johannites, venerates John the Baptist more highly than it does Jesus. The sect lives on into the present day, mostly in Iraq.

ARIANISM: Said to have come from Egypt in the 3rd century, Arianism opposed the concept of the Holy Trinity. Jesus and God were not the same, it claimed, thus calling Jesus' divinity into question. Arianism was the predominant Christian sect in Western Europe until the 6th century: among its adherents were the Merovingian kings of France. The Carolingians who supplanted them were aligned with the Church of Rome.

MANICHAEISM: Attributed to a 3rd-century Persian prophet but having far older roots, Manichaeism proposed that good and evil were of equal power. The material world was evil ("lord of this world" becoming one of the titles of Satan), and the spiritual world was good. Such dualism was common among early Christian heresies, and it called into question the Catholic position that God is all-powerful and his priests can redeem all things.

CATHARISM: A Gnostic-dualist sect, the Cathars became widespread throughout the Languedoc (today's southern France) and adjoining areas of Spain and Italy in the 12th century. Their beliefs also spread into northern France and Germany. The main charges against the Cathars were: they denied the Eucharist (the transubstantiation of the communion wafer into the literal body of Christ); they believed that water, being material and therefore spiritually impure, could not purify anything (making the sacrament of baptism useless); they did not believe that priests had the authority to absolve sins; and they opposed the veneration of the cross.

The Council of Vienne in 1311 formally absolved the Templars of heresy, which was the most credible of the charges against them. (Classic Image / Alamy)

The Charges

Many of the charges leveled against the Templars can be explained in terms of religious rituals that the Church of Rome regarded as heretical. Examining the charges one by one, Fouchet makes a powerful argument for the existence of a Templar Creed which united many heresies into a new, non-Catholic form of Christianity.

The Cross

One can only imagine the horror with which Catholic Europe viewed the charge that Templar rituals involved trampling and spitting upon the cross. Such a practice would indeed be contrary to everything that the Church of Rome stood for, but it is not incompatible with the beliefs of other groups, arguably no less Christian, which might have influenced Templar thinking.

The Mandaeans dismissed Jesus altogether as a religious figure, believing that John the Baptist was the Messiah for whom the Jewish race had been waiting. Thus, according to some scholars, they would regard the cross as irrelevant at best, and at worst as the symbol of a false prophet. Defiling the cross might be a symbolic act demonstrating attachment to Mandaean beliefs.

Also interesting is the widespread belief among the Arians, the Gnostics, and the Cathars that Jesus was entirely mortal. According to some accounts he died on the cross and there was no resurrection; according to others (including the Nag Hammadi scrolls) a lookalike named Simon of Cyrene was crucified instead and the resurrection was a hoax. While it is true that many Gnostic and other sects regarded the crucifixion – and the cross itself – as irrelevant, would any of them entertain the kind of sustained hostility toward it that the Templars allegedly displayed? It seems unlikely, and the only evidence for such rituals comes from the Catholic Church itself, in accusations against the Templars and other alleged heretics.

However, hatred of the cross is not the only possible interpretation of this ritual, if it ever occurred. The cross is, of course, the instrument of Jesus' execution as well as the symbol of his sacrifice. It is possible that by defiling the cross the Templars symbolized their resolve to undo the crucifixion and establish an earthly kingdom of God in the newly Christian Jerusalem.

Some Gnostic and neo-Platonic writings hint that a ritual of standing upon the cross was a form of mystical initiation, symbolizing a spiritual ascent from the material world and into a higher realm of spirit. Many of the documents regarding the Templar trials mention secrecy and secret rituals, and Fouchet points out that mystical initiations are used by many groups including the Freemasons and the Assassins.

There are two main reasons why levels of initiation might have been a part of the Templar Creed: one mystical and one practical.

The Templar Creed was based on beliefs and documents that had been suppressed by the Church of Rome for centuries. Some of its precepts would have been extremely disturbing to a medieval individual who had been raised on Catholic teachings. The initiate's mind needed to be prepared – or indoctrinated – so that it was ready to receive the new knowledge. The initiate had to be taught to think for himself and to question things that the Church insisted must be taken on faith. Knowledge was passed on only when the initiate's superiors thought he was ready. In addition to being psychologically prepared to receive the forbidden teachings, the initiate also had to prove himself to his superiors. The secrets of the Templar Creed were only passed on to those who had proved themselves loyal and trustworthy. Anyone who leaked the truth to Church authorities – as Squin de Flexian was to do – would place the Order, the Creed, and the whole Templar cause in terrible danger. The Order could not risk outright conflict with Rome until it was securely in command of its own state and could defend itself from a full-scale crusade. If the Templars used a system of mystical initiation as Fouchet suggests, then the majority of the Order would have known little or nothing of the Templar Creed. Those who had proved their loyalty and open-mindedness would have been promoted to higher positions, and with each promotion they would receive more information.

INITIATION DU GRAND ÉCOSSAIS DE SAINT ANDRÉ

A 19th-century image of Freemasons worshiping the Templars' Baphomet idol. Probably Vatican-sponsored propaganda to discredit both groups. (Mary Evans Picture Library / Alamy)

Baphomet

Much has been made, down the centuries, of the name of Baphomet. According to the records of Templar trials, Baphomet was the name of an idol of some kind that played a role in Templar rituals.

Many commentators have rushed to treat Baphomet as a corruption of Mohammed and conclude that the Templars were secret Muslims; however, Islam is even more violently opposed to idolatry than most Christian sects, so it seems impossible that the Templars would have worshipped the Prophet of Islam in the form of an idol.

There is an Arabic word, *bufihamet* or *abufihamet*, which translates as "Father (i.e. 'Source') of Wisdom/Understanding"). Fouchet finds this to be a more likely derivation of Baphomet; it may even refer to the severed head, especially if it was made to speak as part of the ritual.

John the Baptist, it will be remembered, was beheaded by Herod at the behest of the dancer Salome, and his severed head became a sought-after relic over the following centuries. At least seven institutions in Europe and the Middle East claim to have it among their relics. If the Templars had absorbed Johannite ideas during their time in the Middle East, then it is possible that their rituals included a relic or symbol of the severed head.

It is known that the Templars had some dealings with the Assassins. Various sources claim that the founder of the Assassin sect, Hassan Sabah, perpetrated an illusion that a severed head was lying on a dish on the floor of his audience chamber, alive and able to speak. In fact, the head belonged to one of his followers who was standing in a concealed pit. The two halves of the plate were fitted around his neck like a collar, and the liberal quantities of blood disguised the joins. It is not inconceivable that the Templars used a similar illusion as part of some initiation or indoctrination process.

According to Fouchet the other reported form of Baphomet, a cat, may be dismissed as the product of tortured imaginations desperate to satisfy their interrogators. The cat familiar has been an indispensable accessory of witches since the earliest times and to the medieval mind heresy and witchcraft were inseparable.

HALLUCINOGENS

When asked to describe the idol Baphomet by their interrogators, the captured Templars came up with a wide range of answers. Some Templars, indeed, claimed to have seen it shift form, perhaps in response to the question of why descriptions of it varied so widely.

A few historians have seized upon this isolated fact as suggesting that the Templars used some kind of hallucinogenic drugs in their rituals – drugs of whose existence they may have learned from the Arab world, and whose use by shamans across the world was not commonly known in medieval Europe. Fouchet comments drily that it is perhaps significant that at least one such historian was writing in the late 1960s.

The Sacraments

The Templars were accused of "scorning" the sacraments of the Catholic Church, "especially confession and penance." This accords with what is known of Gnostic and Cathar beliefs, strengthening the suggestion that the Templars had been influenced by such doctrines at some point in their history.

Fouchet's notes point out that it is also possible to interpret this charge in a different light. It is known that the Templars showed no reluctance to recruit members who had been excommunicated by the Church; some writers have gone so far as to suggest that this was a deliberate policy, at least in some times and places. Once inducted into the Order, these men were permitted to receive penance and absolution from the Order's chaplains, despite their excommunicate status. It is quite possible that the charge refers to this practice; by offering them to those who had been excommunicated, the Templars made a mockery of the sacraments in the Church's eyes.

However the Templars actually scorned the sacraments of Rome, it is certain that they would have found many willing and potentially loyal recruits among the excommunicate. Having renounced the Church by joining the Order, these individuals would have been more open to receiving the teachings of the Templar Creed than recruits who remained devout Catholics.

Muslim Sympathies

Based on the spurious Baphomet–Mohammed link, the Templars' known dealings with the Assassins, and other factors, it has been suggested that the Templars were secret Muslims, or Muslim sympathizers, who had conspired to place the Holy Land back in Muslim hands. There were some who blamed the Order for the loss of the Holy Land after the disasters of the Second Crusade, and not without reason. It was the Templar Grand Master Gerard de Rideford, by all accounts, who urged the disastrous attack at Hattin that precipitated the almost complete collapse of the Crusader states.

At the time of the Templar trials, almost any interest in eastern forms of Christianity could be interpreted in Europe as a sympathy with Islam. Although the question of Gnostic and other influences remains unresolved, there is no persuasive evidence that the Order embraced Islam in any way.

Other commentators have seized upon the Templar's dealings with the Assassins and their easy relationship with their Jewish and Muslim neighbors in Outremer to suggest that they had become more familiar with Jews and Muslims than was seemly for good Christians. Fouchet's work points to a deliberate plan to unite all the religions of the Middle East in a pan-Abrahamic religion independent of both the Catholic and Orthodox Churches.

The Grail's Journey

From the fall of Acre in 1291, the Grail was almost continually on the move. It was initially kept in Templar-owned buildings in Jerusalem, and progressively evacuated as the Crusader states fell. It was moved to Cyprus before the siege of Acre, and de Molay worked to prepare a new generation of Templar leaders to replace those who had died in the siege.

De Molay planned an attack on Syria but failed to win a foothold in the Holy Land. He turned back to Cyprus, but the Templars were caught up in a local power struggle and the island remained as ungovernable as ever. De Molay ordered the Grail moved to the Temple in Paris as he struggled to find a way forward for the Templar enterprise.

Worse news came when Pope Clement warned de Molay about Philip IV's plans to attack the Order. He had the treasure moved to Scotland and was arrested soon after it left.

The magical texts, if they could be attributed to a biblical figure like Solomon, challenged the Church line that miracles were reserved for God and the saints, and all magic was therefore heretical.

The philosophical and religious texts, which included many gospels excluded from the Bible by earlier Church councils, offered a different point of view that could be used by heretical groups like the Cathars to challenge Church teachings.

When the arrests and confiscations of 1307 failed to deliver Solomon's library, the Church made every effort to track down and seize or suppress any document that might be a part of it. In 1351, Pope Innocent VI ordered a grimoire called *The Book of Solomon* to be seized and burned, and others followed. Especially targeted was a work called *The Key of Solomon* whose origins can be traced back to the Italian Renaissance.

According to Fouchet, this work was another "false Grail" created by the surviving Templars to cover the trail of Solomon's library. It contained just enough truth to convince Church authorities that it was genuine, and was distributed widely across Europe to distract the Inquisitors from the Templars' real plans.

Scotland

The Order had deep roots in Scotland. Hugues de Payens had personally met with King David I in 1128. Henry St Clair, the second baron of Roslin, had served with de Payens in the First Crusade and may have provided an introduction. Over the next 184 years the Order founded preceptories in Scotland and accumulated a great deal of land there, just as it did in other countries.

The fact that Scotland was excommunicated in 1312 prevented the promulgation there of Pope Clement's bull officially dissolving the Order. However, some trials did take place in Scotland. Officially, the Templars in Scotland were dissolved, as they were in England, by order of King Edward II. However, Scotland had its own king at the time, Robert the Bruce, and it is far from clear whether the English king's pronouncements were taken seriously.

It has been claimed, though never proven, that Templar knights fought on the Scottish side at the Battle of Bannockburn in 1314. If this is true, then the Templars must have been on good terms with the Scottish crown – perhaps even under its protection – which makes it unlikely that any serious efforts were made to suppress the Order in Scotland.

Officially, at least, the Templars' lands and possessions in Scotland were transferred to the Hospitallers, as, most likely, were many of the Templars themselves. Another unproven rumor asserts that the Templars and Hospitallers merged to form a new order, named the Order of St John and the Temple, which, if true, implies that the Scottish Templars kept at least some of their prestige. This Order is claimed to have lasted until its last preceptor Sir James Sandilands converted to Protestantism in 1553.

Rumors of Templar activity in Scotland persisted. The 18th-century French monk and chronicler Dom Augustin Calmet claimed that Viscount Dundee, who fought on the Stuart side at the Battle of Killiecrankie in 1689, was a Templar Grand Master and that the Grand Cross of the Order was found on his body after he fell.

PRINCE ZICHMNI

In 1558, a Venetian named Niccolo Zeno published a book which he claimed was based on letters and a map handed down from his ancestors Niccolo and Antonio Zeno, who lived around 1400. The book describes a voyage the brothers took around 1398 across the North Atlantic to Greenland. The expedition was under the command of a prince named Zichmni: some have claimed that this Zichmni was actually Henry Sinclair (a British variant of the Norman St Clair), the first baron of Roslin, who died around 1400.

The authenticity of the Zeno letters has long been disputed, as has the identification of the mysterious Prince Zichmni with Henry Sinclair. Defenders of the Zeno narrative have suggested that the name arose from a misreading of the original manuscript's attempt to spell Orkney, perhaps as "d'Orchani." Sinclair was the earl of Orkney at that time, and given the map's medieval writing style the word "d'Orchani" could be mistaken for "Zichmni."

A letter of 1745 from the duke of Perth to the earl of Airlie describes a ceremony in which Bonnie Prince Charlie became the Grand Master of the Templars after his victory over the English at Prestonpans. Fouchet believed he was a Freemason and not a Templar. Many leading Jacobites were Freemasons; the claim that the prince was a Mason has been dismissed by English lodges, but is supported by Scottish ones.

Was Poussin's painting a hint pointing to the New World? (PD-US)

Roslin

According to Fouchet, the lost Templar fleet crossed the English Channel and went up the coast to the Firth of Forth. From there, a short journey up the River Esk led to within yards of Roslin. The famous Rosslyn Chapel had not yet been built, but the St Clair family of Roslin provided refuge for a time.

After a few years, though, it became clear that constant English pressure made Scotland too dangerous. Using contacts in the Order of Teutonic Knights, the Grail's guardians took ship from Scotland and followed old Viking sea-routes to Norway, Iceland, and the ailing Norse Greenland colony before traveling south from Greenland in search of Vinland. There, in modern-day Quebec, the Grail's guardians founded a kingdom that the native Iroquois called Saguenay.

It seems likely that Roslin remained a key link in a secret Templar network that extended from Europe to North America. Rosslyn Chapel's decorative stonework includes some apparent images of uniquely North American plants, including maize.

THE FREEMASONS

The Freemasons are the most prominent of several societies that claim to be descended from the Templars. Several degrees of Masonic initiation have titles that refer to the Knights Templar.

Evidence for the early history of Freemasonry is sparse. The architecture of Rosslyn Chapel, built in the mid-15th century, contains several elements which have been interpreted as Masonic symbols. By 1535, two Scottish Masonic lodges are recorded at Paris and Lyon.

In 1602, Sir William St Clair of Roslin was granted the right of patronage over the Masons of Scotland. The esoteric side of Freemasonry became more pronounced from this point on.

From 1717, Freemasonry became more open about its existence. Either it spread rapidly throughout Europe and North America, or established lodges dropped their veil of secrecy.

The Devil supporting the font in the church at Rennes-le-Château. Details like this have fed the appeal of the "Plantard plot" but are probably deliberate misdirection. (Leslie Garland Picture Library / Alamy)

Saguenay

According to Fouchet's research the kingdom of Saguenay was founded on the Gulf of St Lawrence in 1322. The Templars in Europe were scattered. Many were dead, and many more were hiding in other military orders. Cut off from contact with Europe, the Templars of Saguenay waited for word of the next plan, but none came.

Saguenay was rich by European standards. Along with the precious documents from Solomon's library, the Templars had brought a king's ransom in gold and jewels, and had the alchemical knowledge to create much more. However, they were few in number and their Algonquin neighbors had no use for gold. The Templars of Saguenay weathered several attacks before a watchful and uneasy truce was concluded.

What news they had of Europe came from northern Europe via Greenland. They heard nothing of Portugal's Knights of Christ, and the Portuguese Templars knew nothing of Saguenay. When the Greenland colony failed in the early 15th century, contact with Europe was disrupted, but not lost altogether.

New France

It was more than a century before Europeans came to the area again. The Templars of Saguenay watched as the first French trading posts gave way to the colony of Acadia, and they melted into the growing population, intending to hide in plain sight. However, this was no easy task.

Although most of Europe thought of the Templars as an extinct medieval phenomenon, the Vatican had a longer memory. Iroquois legends of Saguenay reached the ears of French missionaries who reported back to Rome. The Inquisition sent agents to investigate, and so did the Hospitallers, who were now known as the Knights of Malta. Both suspected that the lost Templar fleet had somehow reached the New World. The Inquisitors wanted to complete the extermination of the Templar heresy and the Knights wanted to get their hands on the Templar treasure that had been granted to them when Pope Clement dissolved the Order.

As the 16th century gave way to the 17th, another group joined the hunt. The Compagnie du Saint-Sacrement had come to New France to hunt Protestant Huguenots, but once its agents became aware of a possible Templar treasure in North America, their attentions shifted.

However, the Templars had been careful. Although several sites on the eastern seaboard of North America are associated with the Templars in local tradition, no trace of the kingdom of Saguenay has ever been found. How could a European community exist in North America for 200 years and remain undetected to the present day? Fouchet believed it could, for three reasons.

First, the groups would probably have been small. Only 50 horsemen left Paris along with the Grail, and even if more Templars joined the group in Scotland the entire expedition could not have consisted of more than a few dozen men.

Second, the settlement of New France was a piecemeal, haphazard undertaking, especially in the early years. It would have been easy enough for a group of Templars to melt into the new colonial population. Given good intelligence about the plans of the Inquisition, the Knights of Malta, and the Compagnie, it would be possible to disperse the true Grail between a number of safe houses and secretly move any part of it that seemed in danger of discovery.

Third, Fouchet points out, there is the magical library of Solomon. Although its exact contents are unknown to anyone except its immediate guardians, the library's reputation is so great that it must surely be able to provide any number of magical resources that would help the Templars and their treasure remain undetected.

Interestingly, the name Arcadia appeared in a trio of enigmatic paintings created in the few decades after the colony's establishment. Nicolas Poussin painted two, including the best known, and the Italian painter Guercino painted one; all show a group of shepherds contemplating a tomb which bears the Latin inscription *Et in Arcadia Ego* – "Even in Arcadia I [am present]." Death is everywhere, even in paradise.

(OVERLEAF) Although most scholars dismiss the Kingdom of Saguenay as an empty legend, Fouchet disagreed, postulating that the Templars established their colony in 1322. Despite hardship, and constant conflict with the Native American tribes, the colony survived and flourished in the time before other European colonization in North America.

Modern conspiracy theorists believe the paintings – especially Poussin's version from 1637–38 – incorporate a coded message that may point to a Templar treasure. The authors of *The Holy Blood and the Holy Grail* suggest the inscription is an anagram: *I Tego Arcana Dei* translates from Latin as "Begone! I cover/conceal the secrets of God." Poussin is said to have boasted that he knew secrets that even kings could not drag from him.

A tomb identical to the one in Poussin's painting exists outside a village called Arques, not far from Rennes-le-Château in the heart of Cathar country. In 1891 the priest of Rennes-le-Château, François Bérenger Saunière, discovered four parchments hidden in a hollow column while engaged in a modest church restoration project. Shortly afterward he went to Paris and acquired a copy of Poussin's painting.

From then until his death in 1917, Saunière spent untold sums of money on an array of local building projects, many times more than he could possibly have earned as a priest. It was commonly believed that the parchments had led him to a lost Cathar or Templar treasure; possibly the painting contained the final clue to its whereabouts.

Bérenger Saunière and Rennes-le-Château went on to play a major role in the Plantard plot, as will be seen later in this book.

The Thirteen Colonies

Even so, with such determined searchers wielding the full resources of the Church, the Grail was no longer safe in New France. Protestant Britain had established 13 North American colonies, two of which were particularly known for their religious tolerance and free-thinking ways: Rhode Island and Pennsylvania.

Around 1690, the Grail was moved to the town of Newport in Rhode Island, where it was kept in the base of an old windmill owned by the governing Arnold family. However, rumors of Templar activity soon leaked out into the town, and it was necessary to move the Grail to a more remote location.

The Pennsylvania Colony was the next choice. Founded by Quakers, it was still a haven for free thought, especially in the progressive city of Philadelphia. Fearing a repeat of events at Newport, the Templars chose a site outside the city. The Grail was hidden some 20 miles away in New Hope township, at the home of a retired physician and Templar agent named John Bowman.

As the 18th century proceeded, Philadelphia became a center of enlightened thinking. Scientific, philosophical, and political thought flourished, as well as mystical research. Philadelphia also became a center of Masonic activity. When friction between the American colonists and the British Parliament came to a head in the 1770s, the framers of the United States Constitution were significantly influenced by the Templar concept of the enlightened state, whether they knew it or not.

The Freemasons played a much more prominent role than the Templars in the American Revolution. Despite their professed reverence for Templar

A strange tower in Newport, Rhode Island may have Templar links. (PD-US)

secrets, the Masons – especially the more mystically inclined "Modern" wing of the movement – regarded the secrets of the Holy Grail as their birthright. At some time in the early 18th century, Masonic agents had located the treasure that Bowman guarded and taken possession of it. Based on his interpretation of several local legends surrounding New Hope and Bowman's Hill, Fouchet even speculated that Freemasons might have been behind Bowman's death.

Washington's famous crossing of the Delaware took place very close to Bowman's Hill, and Fouchet believed this is not a coincidence. He suggests that Washington could not have moved such a large force, including artillery, across an ice-strewn river in winter without incident unless he had what Fouchet calls "unusual control" over the operation. The complete surprise Washington achieved against seasoned Hessian troops in his attack on Trenton also strikes Fouchet as "straining the normal laws of probability."

Fouchet also points to reports that Washington received a mystical vision of the future of the United States while encamped at Valley Forge in the winter of 1777–78 as evidence that Washington was using the magic of Solomon to bolster the effectiveness of his Continental Army, which was outclassed and outnumbered by the British regulars ranged against it.

The Secret War

Return to Europe

Fouchet was certain that the Grail returned to Europe at some time before 1800. It is almost never seen directly, but its presence, Fouchet believed, can be seen behind a pattern of events over the next two centuries.

Fouchet's theory, briefly, is as follows. With Washington established as the first president of the United States and Freemasons in control of the Grail, word of its existence spread among Masonic groups in Europe. While the American Templars planned an operation to recover the Grail and bring it to Europe, their European counterparts set about preparing the ground there.

When the Inquisition learned that the Grail was in the hands of the Freemasons, the Church reacted vigorously. Since 1314 its war against the Templars had been conducted in secret because the Church could not afford to admit that the Templars still existed; the Freemasons were a much more visible target. Starting with Pope Clement XII's excommunication of all Catholic Freemasons in 1738, anti-Masonic pronouncements issued from the Vatican on a regular basis. The Inquisition began tracking down senior Freemasons across Europe, hoping to uncover a trail that led to the Templars or to the Grail itself.

The Templars took advantage of this conflict, and also of the schism that split Masonry into the Ancient and Modern factions. Templar agents infiltrated the Freemasons at all levels. As well as sowing various "false Grail" documents that were supposed to contain lost Templar secrets, they promoted the formation of even more splinter groups and "strict observances" until Freemasonry threatened to dissolve into a chaos of squabbling subgroups.

At the same time, the Templars encouraged the proliferation of other esoteric groups across Europe and North America. These included the Illuminati, the Rosicrucians, and various organizations whose names included the words "Temple" or "Templar."

George Washington was one of many Freemasons who were active in the American Revolution. (Library of Congress)

These groups were put to various uses at various times. It was not uncommon for a particular group to serve more than one purpose. Some were decoys intended to send the Inquisition on an endless series of snipe hunts. Others were used to weaken the Freemasons by attracting their more esoterically inclined members. Most were also used, at one time or another, to draw in prominent scientists, thinkers, politicians, and nobles, so that their usefulness to the Templars' overall plan could be assessed.

The Grail Recovered

Benjamin Franklin's weakness for wine and women is almost as well known as his connection with Masonic groups on both sides of the Atlantic. He is known to have visited the notorious Hell Fire Club during his visits to England.

During his tenure as American Ambassador to France, Franklin was inducted into a similar organization. Named l'Ordre du Temple, it had been founded at the court of Louis XIV as a secret society whose object was "the pursuit of pleasure." On the surface at least, it had been reformed by the duke of Orleans in 1705 and given an elaborate false Templar history. Templar agents within this group induced Franklin to give up the Grail's location, and it was quickly recovered and smuggled back to Paris. How they did so is a matter for speculation, but Franklin's temperament made him vulnerable to alcohol, sex, and magic, all of which the Order had at its disposal.

In the secret war that followed American independence, many organizations claimed dual Templar and Masonic affilitations. It is stil hard to untangle the truth about them. (Library of Congress)

Revolution and the 19th Century

According to Fouchet the whole of French history during what some call "the long 19th century" was the result of a clandestine struggle between the Templars, the Freemasons, and the Inquisition.

The Templars returned the Grail to Europe in the hope of establishing their ideal kingdom in France. They helped bring about the fall of the French Bourbon dynasty and establish the First Republic, but lost control of the situation in the Terror.

The French Revolution

Having seen the success of the American Revolution, the Templars hoped for a similar result in France. However, the high ideals of the early Revolution quickly gave way to the intrigue and violence of the Terror. Fouchet regarded it as significant that the Paris Temple, once the Templars' world headquarters, was chosen to hold the royal family pending their execution, and that the official name for Louis XVI became "Citizen Louis Capet" – a reference to the now-extinct dynasty of their old enemy Philip le Bel.

At first, the Revolution served to protect the Templars and the Grail from the Church, which was hard-pressed to deal with a number of Revolutionary laws that weakened the Vatican's links to the French clergy by making them all employees of the state. The Freemasons, whose membership in France consisted almost entirely of noblemen, were similarly distracted. The Templars pressed their advantage and began to shape Revolutionary ideals toward establishing an "illuminated" state like those they had tried to create in Jerusalem, Cyprus, and the Languedoc.

The Templars' campaign almost succeeded. In 1792, the last serious threat was removed when Maximilien de Robespierre forced the Marquis de Lafayette, the French hero of the American Revolution and a powerful Freemason, to flee France. But Robespierre's victory made him overconfident. Backed up by the dreaded Committee of Public Safety, he forced through a program of change that was far too aggressive.

Fouchet believed that Robespierre had been destabilized by the Freemasons. They had infiltrated the Jacobin party of which Robespierre was a prominent member, and in many parts of France new Jacobin clubs grew out of existing Masonic lodges. Rather than trying to take over the Revolution, though, the Freemasons made sure it was doomed.

Fouchet was uncertain whether Robespierre's planned Republic of Virtue and religion of the Supreme Being were originally Templar ideas. Robespierre's brutal urgency in using the Terror as an instrument of social change clearly was not. The Templars were unable to rein him in, and Robespierre was executed for tyranny in 1794. A victim of the brutal system he had helped establish, he received no trial.

It was clearly too dangerous to keep the Holy Grail in Paris after this. Although the violence of the Revolution was widespread throughout the country, the south had escaped the worst excesses. The Templars moved the Grail to Toulouse, but in 1799 an attack by British and Spanish royalist armies forced another move, to the fortified town of Rennes-le-Château some 75 miles away.

Rennes-le-Château

Rennes-le-Château was part of a chain of forts that guarded the French side of the Pyrenees. The entire region had been devastated during the Albigensian Crusade, and again several centuries later when the French monarchy tried to stamp out Protestantism in the area. Cathar roots and distrust of Paris both ran deep here.

The exact hiding-place of the Grail at Rennes-le-Château is not known. The village priest, Antoine Bigou, fled to Spain during the Revolution, leaving several clues to the Grail's location hidden in the church. These would not be found for almost a century.

Napoleon

After Robespierre's downfall, the Templars began to groom a young Corsican artillery officer named Napoleon Bonaparte. His First Empire was to have been the foundation of an enlightened monarchy along Templar lines.

Bonaparte reimposed order across France. He patronized l'Ordre du Temple (see p.58) and may have been a member. During his campaigns in Italy, Napoleon had huge quantities of documents removed from the Vatican and elsewhere and brought to Paris for study, along with the "false Grail" from Genoa. When these materials were returned to Rome in 1815, over 2,000 documents were lost or missing.

Fouchet was convinced that the main goal of this project was to recover everything possible that had been lost during the raids of October 1307. Fouchet also believed that Napoleon was looking for the Grail on his own account. With its power, he could rule unfettered by any allegiance to the Templars.

Fouchet believed that the Grail was kept hidden in Rennes-le-Château until late in the 19th century, precisely so that none of the Templars' potential puppet rulers would try to seize it for themselves.

On Napoleon's orders, the Paris Temple was demolished in 1808. Outmoded as a fortress, it was now a symbol and place of pilgrimage for French royalists because Louis XVI and Marie Antoinette had been imprisoned there. To refurbish it would have been to show the Templars' hand far too plainly, and the Order did not want pro-Bourbon royalists destabilizing the First Empire.

Having pacified and organized France, Napoleon turned his attention to Europe. Despite many brilliant victories, his forces were ground down by a succession of alliances. His defeat at the Battle of Waterloo in 1815 and his exile to St Helena brought the First Empire to an end. A Bourbon monarchy was reinstated in France, with far more restrictions on its power than before. As the Inquisition and the Freemasons fought for control of the new French monarchy, the Templars turned elsewhere.

The Paris Temple became a prison until it was demolished on Napoleon's orders. (INTERFOTO / Alamy)

The Habsburgs

John B. Morris photographed in the 1860s in full masoic or templar regalia. Many well respected gentlemen of this time period were members of lodges and secret societies, but what role most of them played in the larger secret war, if any, has been lost to history. (Library of Congress)

Failure in Cyprus and the Languedoc had taught the Templars not to put all their eggs in one basket. A European Templar group had been cultivating the Habsburgs since taking refuge in the east in the early 14th century. In return for its protection, the Templars had helped the House of Habsburg to grow into a major power, counting Holy Roman Emperors and kings of Austria among its progeny. By the early 19th century the Habsburgs controlled the thrones of Austria, Spain, and Portugal, and were the only European dynasty more powerful than the Bourbons. No other power on earth could unite Europe into an ideal Templar state.

In 1848 the Freemasons fomented a number of local rebellions across Habsburg territory with the intention of destabilizing their empire. When the unrest spread to France, the Templars turned it to their advantage and replaced the Inquisition-backed Bourbon monarchy with the Second Republic.

Under Napoleon III, this became the Second Empire. It was a diversion, and the Freemasons were deceived. They had gained control of the Hohenzollern family that ruled Prussia, and goaded France into a series of wars that brought down the Second Empire and saw it replaced by a Third Republic. The Templars made token efforts to resist Masonic domination of the new republic, and the Freemasons became convinced that Templar power was all but spent – but in truth, their main efforts were directed toward the Habsburgs.

L'ORDRE DU TEMPLE

In 1804, the same year he crowned himself Emperor, Napoleon supported the foundation of a neo-Templar organization called l'Ordre du Temple. It is not clear whether this was a continuation of the earlier group of the same name, or whether it was a new organization with the same name. Eight years later the Order's founder, Bernard-Raymond Fabré-Palaprat, founded l'Église Johannites des Chrétiens Primitif (The Johannite Church of Primitive Christians); it will be remembered that the heresy charges against the Templars included several that suggested Johannite beliefs.

Today, the Ordo Supremus Militaris Templi Hierosolymitani (OSMTH), also known as Knights Templar International, claims descent from Fabré-Palaprat's order. l'Église Johannite des Chrétiens Primitifs also survives. Both are active in multiple countries across Europe and North America.

Fouchet speculated that the Johannite Church was somehow linked to the Templar Creed and the "bearded head" the Templars were said to worship. His notes indicate that he suspected both the church and the order of having genuine Templar links.

Fouchet was also intrigued by the fact that 14 citizens of Troyes, a city so prominent in the Templars' early history, received patents of nobility and coats of arms from l'Ordre du Temple. Fouchet made his fatal trip to that city in order to search the ducal archives of Champagne for any trace of either organization or any sign that the "Troyes cabal" had survived into the present day.

Rennes-le-Château

All this time, both the Inquisition and the Freemasons had been trying to discover where the Grail was hidden. Of all the Inquisition's agents and informants, the one who came closest to finding the Grail was François Bérenger Saunière, the priest of Rennes-le-Château. His efforts earned him a fictional place in the Plantard plot as an agent of the Priory of Sion.

Starting in 1887, Saunière embarked on a program of building and restoration that neither he nor the parish could possibly afford. This construction, secretly funded by the Inquisition, covered a frantic program of excavations sparked by the recovery of the documents hidden in the church by Antoine Bigou.

Saunière's project brought many workers to the village, and Fouchet believed that among them were Templar agents who managed to spirit the Grail to safety without arousing suspicion. The Templars leaked several documents referring to the village, convincing both the Inquisition and the Freemasons that the Grail was still close by, and creating a period of confusion as the Inquisition and the Freemasons fought a secret battle in the area.

Fouchet concluded that the Inquisition won the struggle, since Saunière's building work continued until 1905. However, all his work and all the Church's expenditure came to nothing. Faced with the problem of closing the project down without raising questions as to how it was funded, the Inquisition made Saunière their scapegoat. In 1911 an ecclesiastical court found him guilty of selling indulgences and he was suspended from the priesthood.

THE KINGS OF JERUSALEM

Fouchet believed that the Templars saw the Habsburgs as more than simply another tool to be discarded if their plans went awry. Over the centuries of its rise to power, the House of Habsburg had accumulated many lands and titles, but most significant of all, he believed, was the fact that the family had a long-standing claim to the lost Crusader kingdom of Jerusalem.

When the Templars fell in 1307 the king of Jerusalem was Henry II, the king of Cyprus. Through his line, and with secret Templar support, the Christian claim to the throne of Jerusalem passed through the houses of Savoy, Anjou, and Lorraine to the Habsburg dynasty, where it resided at the time the Grail returned to Europe in the late 18th century.

Over the intervening centuries, two competing claims had arisen through the labyrinth of European dynastic politics. The weakest of these was from the Italian House of Savoy, and was never pressed. A stronger challenge came from the Spanish House of Bourbon, which had links to the fallen Capetian dynasty of Philip le Bel.

Given these facts, Fouchet argues, it is natural that the Templars should take a deep and abiding interest in the fortunes of the House of Habsburg. He even wondered whether the Order still planned to make Jerusalem the capital of its planned empire once it had united Europe. Even today, the only hope for bringing peace to the Middle East lies in reconciling the religious differences between Christians, Jews, and Muslims, and Fouchet's conclusions about the Templar Creed make it quite plausible that this is the next step in the Order's ambitious plan.

The "Angels of Mons" appeared on the battlefields of World War I. Were they the result of Templar magic as some have claimed? (Mary Evans Picture Library / Alamy)

Although he was certain that the Grail was moved from Rennes-le-Château, Fouchet was unable to discover where it went. His notes indicate that he thought l'Ordre du Temple may have been involved and that the Grail was moved either to Troyes or to Sion in Switzerland.

The Great War

While the Freemasons were distracted by their efforts to destroy the Second Empire, the main Templar effort saw the Habsburg-ruled Austro-Hungarian Empire grow into Europe's greatest power. In June 1914, the Habsburg Archduke Franz Ferdinand of Austria was assassinated by a Bosnian student named Gavrilo Princip; Fouchet's notes indicate that he had not yet examined the common claim that the Freemasons were somehow involved. Following that assassination, the Freemasons orchestrated a groundswell of anti-German and anti-Austrian sentiment across Europe. Nation after nation entered the Great War as governments were unable to resist the will of their people.

Fouchet noted that several possibly occult events took place during the war, the most famous being the incident of the "Angels of Mons." His notes suggest that he intended to investigate these reports later and determine if Templar magic had been involved in any of them. He was unable to do so before his death, but he clearly believed that the secret war continued on the battlefield.

After four years, the Austro-Hungarian Empire was in ruins and Habsburg fortunes were at their lowest ebb. However, the Templars were not ready to write off the investment they had made in this great house.

Between the Wars

It took the Templars more than 30 years to recover from this setback. The Freemasons had free run of Europe and consolidated their position. The Inquisition was dealing with the Catholic Church's loss of power and prestige in the industrial era, and its operations were severely curtailed as the Church strove to retain its power in the period between the First and Second Vatican councils.

It was at this time that a sinister fourth player entered the game. Even before the Great War, German occultists had been systematically searching for the Templars and their secrets. Romantic poets and composers such as Richard Wagner had tied the Grail romances into a growing German national mythology, and their work attracted the attention of several men who would become leading members of the National Socialist Party. As Germany struggled to recover its sense of national self-esteem in the aftermath of defeat, the National Socialists grew in power.

At first, the Inquisition saw the rise of the Christian Socialist Party in Austria as an opportunity to wrest control of the Habsburgs away from the Templars. However, as the Austrian party grew closer and closer to its German counterpart, the Church found itself in a difficult position – marginalized at best, and at worst complicit in policies that were counter to its interests.

The Nazis and the Grail

To most Nazis, the imagery of the Templars and that of the Holy Grail were nothing more than nationalist icons adapted to serve the Party's agenda, much like the swastika and the SS "sieg" rune taken from Norse tradition and the black cross of the Teutonic Knights that emblazoned German tanks and aircraft. But to a small elite within the Party, these things were real and powerful.

Nazi Grail hunters have been covered in more detail in another volume in this series, *The Nazi Occult* by Kenneth Hite. After the fall of France, German troops conducted excavations in and around the village of Rennes-le-Château, but the Grail had already been moved by the Templars. In fact, Fouchet believed that it was moved after the murder of Antoine Gélis in 1897 (see p.62), but his notes contain no hint as to where it was taken.

The Plantard Plot

During World War II the regrouped Templars encouraged an ultranationalist publisher named Pierre Plantard, and through the 1950s he published a series of documents relating to the Priory of Sion, an alleged offshoot of the Templars that was the guardian of a secret bloodline that ran from Jesus and Mary Magdalene through the Merovingian dynasty to Plantard himself. The "Plantard plot," as Fouchet calls it, gained some believers in France through the 1960s and 1970s, but became a worldwide sensation in 1982 with the publication of the book *The Holy Blood and the Holy Grail.*

The Last Supper by Leonardo da Vinci plays a key role in *The Da Vinci Code*, a developed form of the Plantard plot which Fouchet believed was a Templar "false Grail." (World History Archive / Alamy)

(OVERLEAF) One of the main charges levelled against the Templars by the church was the use of black magic. The summoning, binding, and questioning of demons has long been thought to be a way of learning secrets and gaining power.

The Plantard plot has now been exposed as a complete fabrication. Fouchet believed it was another "false Grail" intended to divert attention away from Templar activities elsewhere. He speculates that one of its goals was to keep Templar-hunters focused on Rennes-le-Château and its environs, and away from the Grail's new hiding place.

A key element in the Plantard plot is the Priory of Sion, a fabricated organization that Plantard and his followers claimed had created the Templars and guarded the secret of the Grail. Those who took the claim seriously looked for the origin of the Order's name in the Holy Land, but Fouchet's notes link it to the town of Sion in Switzerland. He believed that either Sion was where the Grail was taken when it was moved from Rennes-le-Château in 1897, or it was the end of a false trail concocted at this time.

THE MURDER OF ANTOINE GÉLIS

Antoine Gélis was the priest of the village of Coustaussa. He was a miser, and according to local gossip he hoarded great wealth in his home. On the night of October 31, 1897 he was tortured and murdered. His home was ransacked and papers were found strewn everywhere, but his money was left untouched. His assailants were never identified.

Fouchet believed that Gélis was murdered by Masonic agents who thought he was the guardian of the Grail. The Inquisition, he wrote, would have taken a more subtle approach. He would have been called to Rome or Toulouse and the Church would have announced that the 70-year-old priest had died before being able to return to his parish. According to Fouchet, Gélis could well have been an agent of the Inquisition, searching for the Grail himself.

The Templars Today

Fouchet's notes give only a slight indication of what he believed the Templars are doing in the present day; they consist of notes to himself on avenues for further research and reports of incidents he intended to investigate. However, once I began to piece them together, their implications were profound.

If Fouchet is to be believed, the secret war of the last two centuries continues unabated, and the Templars are growing ever closer to realizing their plan for a paneuropean – possibly global – state ruled by priest-kings in the Solomonic tradition. The Freemasons and the Inquisition continue to oppose them, each for their own reasons.

Operations against the Vatican

Although the Templars potentially recovered up to 2,000 lost documents from the Vatican during the reign of Napoleon, Fouchet believed that Templar agents have been actively involved in a campaign to plunder both the Vatican's secret archives and the archive of the Congregation for the Doctrine of the Faith, which before 1904 was known as the Inquisition.

In particular, Fouchet was interested in two burglaries that occurred in 1900 and 1969. The main reason for his interest seems to have been the fact that these two incidents were widely reported.

The Vatican has its own internal police force, and despite the fact that it has one of the highest crime rates in the world compared to its population, crime tends to go unreported in the world media. These two did not. The two break-ins were reported as simple burglaries that gained their perpetrators small amounts of cash and other valuables, but Fouchet believed that there was more to them. Although it acted too late to prevent news from leaking out, the Vatican took some trouble to play down the significance of these two incidents.

The Vatican's secret archives contain many Templar documents seized in 1307. (Corbis)

1900

In addition to their ongoing efforts to recover mystical and heretical documents from the Church, Fouchet identified two reasons why the Templars should have struck in 1900. The murder of Antoine Gélis was only three years in the past, and the Freemasons and the Inquisition were both focused on the false trail that led to Rennes-le-Château.

The Inquisition might have found something of actual value during their researches in the area, perhaps dating back to the Albigensian Crusade – or the operation could have been a deliberately botched attempt to recover documents found in the area, intended to convince the Inquisition of their authenticity and value.

Also in 1900, the Vatican was engaged in a review and overhaul of the Inquisition, perhaps in direct response to lessons learned during the preceding century of secret war. In 1904 the Inquisition changed its name to the Supreme Sacred Congregation of the Holy Office; other, less visible changes were also made to its structure, organization, and methods of operation. Fouchet speculated whether the burglars were Templar or Freemason agents searching for information on the coming changes.

1969

In August 1969, burglars penetrated the pope's private apartments and allegedly made off with medals and paintings of little value. Two men were arrested for the crime in May 1973.

Fouchet found it significant that the same month, the al-Aqsa Mosque in Jerusalem was damaged in an apparent arson attack. The alleged perpetrator was judged to be insane, but Fouchet speculated that the fire might have been set to cover up a bungled Inquisition search of the Templars' first headquarters.

If the Inquisition did have a research team working in the vicinity of Solomon's Temple, the Templars would have had every reason to be curious about their activities. As a part of the secret war, reports on this operation would have been restricted to the very highest Church officials, including the pope. While admitting that his speculations are impossible to prove, Fouchet wondered whether these documents were the real target of the 1969 burglary.

Also in 1969, the seeds were sown for a financial and political scandal that would shake the Vatican more than a decade later. Members of the Propaganda Due ("P2") Masonic lodge became closely involved with the Vatican Bank, the Italian government, and the Mafia. By the time their activities were exposed, these individuals had risen to positions of enormous influence and effectively constituted a "shadow government." Although claims of Vatican complicity have always been officially denied, Fouchet wondered whether the Templars were aware of these developments and broke into the pope's private apartments seeking evidence of a possible Vatican–Masonic alliance.

The Inquisition

In the last few decades a number of scandals have come to light regarding the Catholic Church and the actions of individual priests and other Church officials. While Fouchet believed that the subject matter of these scandals was entirely genuine, he remarked that the Templars would have benefited from the disruption they caused to the Church and the Inquisition, and suspected that the Order may have had a role in bringing them to light.

The reorganization of 1904 that changed the Inquisition's official name to the Supreme Sacred Congregation of the Holy Office was ineffective, according to Fouchet. Despite repeated papal bulls and other Vatican pronouncements against Freemasonry, the movement continued to grow in both numbers and influence. Although they are much more difficult to trace, Fouchet believed that the Inquisition's efforts to crush the Templars met with a similar lack of success.

Much has been made of the Vatican's official policy of neutrality during World War II. While it is certainly true that the occupation of Rome by German troops during the latter part of the war would have made open resistance difficult, Fouchet thought that the Nazis and the Inquisition had a few common goals at this time – Grail-hunting among them – and regarded it as possible that the two groups co-operated, or at least tried to use each other, during this period.

Pope Pius XII, who had occupied the throne of St Peter during the war, was succeeded by John XXII in 1958. Within three months of his election, John called the Second Vatican Council to address matters of doctrine and help modernize the Church. Fouchet believed that this meeting of over 2,000 senior Church officials from all over the world must have included a large number of unofficial sessions, and that the matter of the Templars and the Grail must have been on their agenda.

The Council lasted from 1960 to 1965. That same year, the Inquisition received another new name – the Sacred Congregation for the Doctrine of the Faith – and another reorganization. Fouchet speculated that this was an effort to deal with repeated Templar infiltration and sabotage.

This anonymous building in New York City houses the headquarters of Opus Dei. (Corbis)

Opus Dei

Fouchet also suspected that the Inquisition secretly took over Opus Dei in 1982 upon the death of its founder, Josemaria Escriva. This secretive organization had been characterized by its critics as a form of "Christian Masonry," and according to Fouchet the Inquisition planned to turn it into a force to combat the Templars and the Freemasons.

Opus Dei became famous in 2003 when it was mentioned in Dan Brown's novel *The Da Vinci Code*. The novel's main content was an updated version of the Plantard plot as set forth 20 years earlier in *The Holy Blood and the Holy Grail*; the addition of Opus Dei was the only significant change. Fouchet's notes indicate that he thought the novel (as well as its even more popular 2006 movie version) was a move by the Templars to expose Opus Dei and render it useless to the Inquisition.

The Swiss Guard was reorganized in 1970 after a Vatican break-in the previous year. (Jeremy Hoare / Alamy)

The Swiss Guard

The renowned Swiss Guard was originally one of three Pontifical Guard forces that protected the Vatican and the pope. The other two, the Palatine Guard and the Noble Guard, were disbanded in 1970. Fouchet believed that the reforming Pope Paul VI reorganized the Pontifical Guard as part of a security review that began about the same time as the Second Vatican Council. The same review led to the reorganization and modernization of the Vatican's internal police force.

During World War II, the Palatine Guard had been involved in confrontations with Italian Fascist forces and occupying German troops. Officially these incidents were mostly sparked by outside attempts to arrest fugitives who were hiding in Vatican buildings; Fouchet believed that on at least some occasions the Guard surprised Nazi Grail-hunters who were trying to break in.

The Noble Guard was originally formed as a cavalry unit, but after 1870 it served as a personal bodyguard for the pope. As such, it would have been responsible for the security of his personal apartments. Fouchet saw its disbandment in 1970 as a direct result of the 1969 burglary. Even if the noble Guard had not actually been infiltrated by the Templars, he argued, its failure to apprehend the burglars clearly demonstrated that it presented no obstacle to their agents.

The Swiss Guard has continued to the present day, but Fouchet believed that it, too, is not without its weaknesses. He points out that the Guard did not prevent the assassination of one pope and an attempt on the life of another, although he did not attribute either attempt to the Templars. In fact, Fouchet suspected the Inquisition of being behind the death of John Paul I, whose moderate leanings were dangerous to the Inquisition's prosecution of the secret war. The attempted assassination of John Paul II in 1981, he believed, was unrelated to the secret war.

In 1998, the Guard's commander and his wife were killed, along with a young guardsman, in what was officially ruled a murder-suicide. While he reserved judgment on the case, Fouchet's notes clearly indicate that he thought it worth investigating further. The official account is so scandalous that he believed it was a cover for a truth that was even more dangerous – such as Templar infiltration of the Swiss Guard or an armed confrontation with Templar agents in the heart of the Vatican.

The "Vatileaks" Scandal

Fouchet's notes include news clippings about a developing scandal that outlived him. Starting in January 2012, Vatican documents were leaked to the Italian press detailing a web of financial corruption that reached to the highest levels. These revelations came hard on the heels of a previous scandal that had led to a criminal investigation of the Vatican Bank on suspicion of money laundering.

The Vatican's internal investigation into the affair was headed by a senior member of Opus Dei. Fouchet's handwritten notes on a news clipping show that he found this choice significant: they read "Opus Dei – administrative arm of Inquisition?"

The Vatican Library holds some 75,000 medieval manuscripts and over 1.1 million printed works. Another 150,000 items are kept in the Vatican's Secret Archives. (Design Pics Inc. / Alamy)

Operations against the Freemasons

In addition to their possible role in exposing the P2 scandal involving Masonic infiltration of the Italian government and the Vatican Bank, Fouchet believed that the Templars have launched other operations to disrupt and weaken the Freemasons worldwide.

In addition to sabotaging Masonic efforts to locate and acquire the Holy Grail, Fouchet believed that since the end of World War II the Templars have been actively involved in breaking Masonic ties to national governments across Europe and the world. He suspected that this effort was part of a larger plan to establish a Templar state – first within the European Union, and then on a broader scale. This objective is discussed in a later section.

The Plantard Plot Expanded

Following the success of *The Holy Blood and the Holy Grail* in the 1980s, the book's authors published a second title, *The Temple and the Lodge,* in 1989. Building on the earlier work, this book claimed to reveal deep and enduring ties between the Templars and the Freemasons. Twenty years later, Dan Brown followed the success of his novel *The Da Vinci Code* with *The Lost Symbol*, which featured a powerful Masonic conspiracy in Washington, DC.

Fouchet believed that each of these new books was, in its own time, intended as a weapon against the Freemasons. While the objective of the original Plantard plot was to sow a false trail and obfuscate the location and nature of the Grail, he wrote, these two books depict the Freemasons as ruthless, scheming powermongers bent on world domination. By focusing attention on the Freemasons, this phase of the plot achieves two objectives: making it more difficult for the Masons to pursue their own goals, and establishing them as convenient scapegoats for any Templar operations that might go awry.

From the 1980s to the present day, a huge body of both literature and fiction has grown up around Masonic conspiracy theories. It runs the gamut from the popular *National Treasure* movies through cable-TV historical exposés to credible journalistic claims of Masonic corruption in various national governments.

While admitting that he was unable to tie this conspiracy trend directly to the Templars, Fouchet observed that it would certainly benefit the Order in carrying out the plans he believed they are pursuing. He also noted that there is a smaller but growing body of alleged Templar lore and conspiracy theory, and wondered whether this represented a Masonic counterattack in kind. If so, he wrote, a campaign was under way for the hearts and minds of readers across the Western world, to paint either the Templars or the Freemasons forever as villains in the public consciousness.

Such an exercise, Fouchet believed, would only be of value to the winner if they planned some significant and overt action in the near future, and if the success of that action depended on carrying public opinion with them – as, for example, a bold political move to advance plans for a supra-national state.

[OVERLEAF] A reconstruction of a Templar break-in at the Vatican library. Fouchet believed that the secret war between the Templars and the Vatican is ongoing, and that both groups control ancient knowledge that the other desires.

Britain

Over the last decade, the British Parliament has seen several attempts to limit Masonic influence in the government of that country.

Against a rising number of accusations that Freemasons in the British government, judiciary, and police forces exchange favors and promote each other's careers, several bills have been introduced that would require British Freemasons to declare their membership upon taking up a post in government or law enforcement. So far the effects of these measures have been limited, in part due to legal challenges made in the European Court.

Fouchet's notes indicate that he believed these British measures were a part of a wider campaign across the European Union and possibly beyond, with the aim of weakening Masonic influence at the highest levels of power. At the time of his death, this line of research was at the top of his list of matters for further inquiry.

The Templar State

The concept of the "Templar State" is central to Fouchet's theory. It has been mentioned in passing elsewhere in this book, but a firm grasp of the idea is necessary to make sense of Fouchet's interpretation of recent Templar activity.

Fouchet's researches convinced him that almost since their founding, the Templars had been involved in various attempts to create an ideal state. It was originally planned to be a new kingdom of Jerusalem that united Christians, Jews, and Muslims under the rule of an enlightened monarch who was part priest and part prophet. Using the wisdom of Solomon and the power of the Holy Grail, this ruler would usher in a new golden age not just for the Holy Land, but for the whole world.

The loss of Acre and the ultimate failure of the Crusades placed Jerusalem out of the Templars' reach for several centuries. In the interim they tried to create an order-state for themselves, first in Cyprus and then in the south of France, but both attempts failed. Driven underground by the pope and the king of France, the Order fled to Scotland and then to North America, guarding its secrets until it felt strong enough to participate in the founding of the United States of America.

Defeated in America by the Freemasons, the Templars returned to Europe and came close to establishing a new state in France. After the failure of this attempt, it was evident that both the Freemasons and the Inquisition would have to be neutralized before any further efforts could be made. Now, after two centuries of planning and preparation, the time is growing near.

That, at least, is the burden of Fouchet's theory. During the last months of his life, he collected a number of news clippings and research materials on the origins and growth of the European Union and on inter-faith relations across Europe and in the Middle East. The information he uncovered is summarized in the remaining pages of this book. Fouchet's comments are included where he left any, but for the most part readers are left, as I was, to form their own conclusions.

The Masonic square and compass on a house in Derbyshire, England. (Alex Ekins / Alamy)

If Fouchet was right in his interpretation of historical and political events, the implications are profound. As it struggles with a Church desperate to retain spiritual authority and the rival Freemasons who are determined to shape the world according to their own designs, the Order of the Knights Templar is actively laying the foundations of a new world order based on religious reconciliation, scientific reason, magical power, and a spiritual authority that has been lost for millennia.

The Habsburgs

Officially, the Habsburg dynasty ended in November 1918 when Charles I stepped down from the thrones of Austria and Hungary. Although their empire was lost, the Habsburgs were still a wealthy and influential family and they had ancestral claims to other territories throughout Europe.

Among the titles still retained by the House of Habsburg was king of Jerusalem. It had been many centuries since this was more than an empty title, but according to Fouchet it explains why the Templars went to so much trouble to cultivate the Habsburgs and ensure their rise to power – and why, even with the Austro-Hungarian Empire destroyed, they did not simply discard the Habsburgs as just another failed tool.

The Habsburgs acquired the Christian claim to Jerusalem in the 18th century. It will also be remembered that the House of Champagne had briefly held the title by marriage in the Templars' early history. Even though no Christian king has sat on the throne of Jerusalem since 1291, the title seems to be of paramount importance to the Templars. Even before the Grail returned to Europe, Templar agents were at work influencing the family's rising fortunes.

Charles I formally stepped down as Austro-Hungarian Emperor after World War I, but Fouchet believed that Templar sponsorship of the Habsburg dynasty continues to this day. (PD-US)

In the aftermath of World War I the Habsburg Emperor Charles I of Austria (also Charles V of Hungary) renounced participation in state affairs, but – significantly according to Fouchet – did not formally abdicate the throne. This led to a persistent Habsburg claim to Austria that was not finally settled until 1961 when Charles' son Otto von Habsburg formally renounced all claims to the throne. However, this did not mean the Habsburgs were a spent political force.

Otto von Habsburg served as a member of the European Parliament, where in a powerful symbolic gesture he had empty seats set up in the European Parliament for representatives from those countries that were on the other side of the Iron Curtain. He also served as vice-president and president of the International Paneuropean Union.

From 1922 to 2000 he was Sovereign of the Austrian Order of the Golden Fleece, whose members include nobles from all over Europe. The membership of the sister Spanish order is even more impressive, including the monarchs of several European countries as well as the president of France, the king of Saudi Arabia, and the emperor of Japan. Although neither branch of the order has any overt links to the Templars, both are in a very strong position to influence European politics.

Two Templars playing chess, from a medieval manuscript. Does the Order continue to use Europe's power elite as pawns? (PD-US)

Fouchet's notes also mention Otto von Habsburg's involvement with the Society of Mont Pelerin and the Three Faiths Forum and point out that the goals of these societies are in keeping with other Templar objectives, namely enlightened rule and the promotion of harmony between Christianity, Judaism, and Islam. Add these to the goal of the Paneuropean Union, Fouchet claimed, and the result is a modern-day equivalent of the Templars' ideal state.

In 2007, Otto von Habsburg passed his titles and offices to his son Karl. After an early career as a broadcaster, Karl carried on his father's political work. He has served in the European Parliament and the United Nations and is the Grand Master of the Order of the Golden Fleece as well as president of the Austrian branch of the Paneuropean Union.

The European Community

The roots of the current European Union go back to the aftermath of World War II. In 1957, the first European Economic Community (EEC) was formed when France, Italy, Germany, Belgium, the Netherlands, and Luxembourg formed an economic partnership under the Treaty of Rome. Among the prime movers in the formation of the EEC was General Charles de Gaulle – who, Fouchet noted, was an alleged correspondent of Pierre Plantard.

Over the next 50 years this organization grew and changed. At the time of writing the European Union, as it is now called, has 27 member states and a supranational parliament which is based in Brussels. Many, but not all, member states use a common currency, the euro, which was introduced in 1998.

The European Union has a population of 500 million people, or just over 7 percent of the world's population. It accounts for approximately 20 percent of the world's gross domestic product, making it the world's largest economy. In a diplomatic coup that Fouchet did not live to see, the organization was awarded the 2012 Nobel Peace Prize in recognition of its contribution "to the advancement of peace and reconciliation, democracy and human rights in Europe."

The balance between European integration and national sovereignty is much debated within the European Union, with great vehemence on both sides. A "United States of Europe" has not been realized, but Fouchet believed that such a superstate would be a significant step along the road to establishing his hypothetical "Templar state." Prominent among the groups calling for closer European integration is the International Paneuropean Union.

The Paneuropean Union

The International Paneuropean Union was founded in 1923 by the son of an Austro-Hungarian diplomat. It was banned by the Nazi government during World War II but was refounded at the war's end. In 1957, the same year that the European Economic Community was founded, Otto von Habsburg became vice-president of the Paneuropean Union. Several European heads of state and other influential people have been members.

A map of the ever-expanding European Union. Are the Templars working to create a supranational state in Europe? (backgrounds / Alamy)

In 1973 Otto von Habsburg became the organization's international president; in the previous year the Plantard plot had been advanced by the broadcast of *The Lost Treasure of Jerusalem ...?* in BBC 2's *Chronicle* documentary series, and by the publication of Donovan Joyce's book *The Jesus Scrolls*. The producers of the BBC program went on to co-author *The Holy Blood and the Holy Grail*.

Fouchet's notes indicate that he found this interesting. If the Plantard plot was indeed a smokescreen intended to direct attention away from Templar activities, then it is significant that the first time it appeared outside France coincided with the rise of a Habsburg to high office in this organization.

In August 1989, the Paneuropean Union organized a protest it called "the Paneuropean Picnic." Amid the widespread protests that preceded the collapse of Communism in eastern Europe, the Paneuropean Union and the opposition Hungarian Democratic Forum organized an event to be held on the Austro-Hungarian border near the town of Sopron. A border gate was to be symbolically opened for three hours, allowing free passage in either direction. The result was that 600 people fled to the West; less than a month later Hungary opened its borders completely, beginning the fall of the Iron Curtain.

Although the demolition of the Berlin Wall in 1990 is more widely remembered, the Paneuropean Picnic was a significant milestone in the collapse of European Communism and the enlargement of the European Union.

There is no direct evidence linking the Paneuropean Union to the Templars, but in his notes Fouchet points out that the organization's flag is identical to the flag of the European Union, with a red cross superimposed over the central circle. The red cross has a long history as a Templar symbol. He also believed the House of Habsburg's close association with the Paneuropean Union is significant.

Conclusion

As I said in the introduction to this book, Fouchet's conclusions are startling. Could it be possible that the Knights Templar not only survived their formal dissolution but have guarded a powerful mystical secret for 700 years, hiding it behind the image of the Holy Grail? Have they fought a 200-year secret war against the Freemasons and the Catholic Church? Have they manipulated people and nations in a grand experiment to create an ideal state free of religious conflict and guided by enlightened principles? Are they close to realizing the first step in this plan? Readers must come to their own conclusions.

There are many other questions that remain unanswered. Where did the Holy Grail go after it was evacuated from Rennes-le-Château? Of the many contemporary organizations that claim descent from the Templars, which are no more than wishful imitators? Which are smokescreens established by the Templars to throw their enemies off the track? Which are fabrications created by the Freemasons, the Inquisition, or Opus Dei to bring the Templars into disrepute? Which are the creations of hucksters and confidence artists? And which, if any, are truly linked to the Order and its mysterious schemes?

These questions will be difficult to answer, and their answers will doubtless lead to even more questions. After seven centuries underground, the Templars will not allow themselves to be found easily. Fouchet, perhaps, came close to doing so, and perhaps it cost him his life. Inspired to solve the mystery of the "Troyes cabal", he stumbled into a world far darker and more complex than anyone could have anticipated.

Timeline

1099: The First Crusade creates the Christian kingdom of Jerusalem.

1104: After meeting with one or more nobles recently returned from Jerusalem, Count Hugh of Champagne spends four years in the Holy Land with Hugues de Payens.

1114: Count Hugh of Champagne makes a second journey to the Holy Land.

1115: Count Hugh returns to France and founds Clairvaux Abbey, appointing the young Bernard de Fontaines as abbott.

1119: Hugues de Payens and eight companions found the Knights Templar. They are housed in the al-Aqsa Mosque near the site of the Temple of Solomon.

c. **1119–27**: The Templars explore the maze of hidden rooms beneath the Temple Mount, finding the Holy Grail and other treasures.

1124: Count Hugh of Champagne officially joins the Templars.

1128: With the support of Bernard of Clairvaux the Templars receive papal recognition at the Council of Troyes; Hugues de Payens visits Scotland and meets with King David I.

1139: Pope Innocent II exempts the Templars from national laws and the authority of monarchs.

1187: The disastrous Battle of Hattin begins the fall of the Crusader kingdoms.

1192–97: Count Henry of Champagne is king of Jerusalem but dies in suspicious circumstances.

1209–29: The Templars secretly assist the Cathars during the Albigensian Crusade.

1284: Prince Philip of France becomes count of Champagne through marriage.

1285: Prince Philip is crowned Philip IV of France, known as Philip le Bel ("the handsome").

1291: Acre, the last Crusader outpost in the Holy Land, falls to Muslim forces. The Templars move their headquarters to Cyprus.

1303: Acting through the Italian Colonna family, Philip le Bel causes the death of Pope Boniface VIII.

1303–04: Philip le Bel feuds with Pope Benedict XI.

1304: Queen Joan of France dies in childbirth; suspicion falls on her husband Philip le Bel.

1305: Pope Clement V is elected through the influence of Philip le Bel.

1306: Riots in Paris drive Philip le Bel to take refuge in the Paris Temple.

1307: Philip le Bel and Pope Clement V act against the Templars. Arrests and interrogations follow; the Grail is moved to Scotland.

1308: In the Chinon Parchment, Pope Clement V absolves the Templars of heresy.

1311: Pope Clement V summons the Council of Vienne, which also absolves the Templars of heresy.

1312: Pope Clement V formally dissolves the Templars.

1314: Jacques de Molay is burned at the stake; Pope Clement V dies of dysentery 33 days later; Philip le Bel dies eight months later, from either a hunting accident or a stroke. Templars allegedly fight on the Scottish side at the Battle of Bannockburn.

1322: The Grail reaches North America; Templar refugees found the kingdom of Saguenay.

1400: Henry St Clair (Sinclair) of Roslin allegedly travels to Greenland using secret Templar sea-routes.

1602: Sir William Sinclair of Roslin becomes patron of all the Freemasons in Scotland.

1689: Viscount Dundee is killed at the Battle of Killiekrankie; the Templar Grand Cross is allegedly found on his body.

c. **1690**: The Grail is moved to Newport, Rhode Island; rumors of Templar activity compromise its safety.

c. **1700**: The Grail is moved to New Hope township, Pennsylvania.

1705: l'Ordre du Temple is refounded by the duke of Orleans.

1717: Freemasonry enters a period of rapid expansion.

1738: The Church and the Freemasons come into open conflict.

1745: Bonnie Prince Charlie allegedly becomes Grand Master of the Templars; it is more likely that he was a Freemason.

1776: Having found the Grail, Washington crosses the Delaware near New Hope township; the tide of the Revolutionary War begins to turn.

1777–78: While wintering at Valley Forge, Washington has a vision of the future United States, possibly as a result of experimenting with the Grail.

1789–99: The French Revolution: the Templars depose the Bourbon dynasty and try to establish an ideal state in France; the Grail is recovered from the Freemasons and moved to Paris.

1793: Washington lays the cornerstone of the US Capitol while dressed in Masonic regalia.

1794: Former Templar agent Maximilien de Robespierre is executed; the Grail is moved to Rennes-le-Château.

1804: Napoleon founds the First Empire of France.

1809: Napoleon occupies Rome; many documents from the Vatican's secret archive are shipped to France; l'Ordre du Temple is apparently revived under his patronage.

1815: Napoleon is defeated at Waterloo; the Templars turn to the Habsburgs.

1848: The Freemasons stir up rebellions across Habsburg territories.

1887: Bérenger Saunière allegedly discovers hidden documents in the church at Rennes-le-Château.

1897: Antoine Gélis is tortured and murdered near Rennes-le-Château, possibly by Masonic agents; his house and papers are ransacked but his money is left untouched. Shortly afterward the Grail is moved from Rennes-le-Château to an unknown location.

1900: A break-in at the Vatican is played down by Church authorities.

1904: The Inquisition is reorganized and renamed.

1911: Bérenger Saunière is suspended for selling indulgences.

1914–18: World War I destroys the Habsburg Austro-Hungarian Empire.

1940–44: Nazi relic hunters search for the Grail near Rennes-le-Château and elsewhere.

1956: Pierre Plantard files official documents founding the Priory of Sion. This apparently fictitious organization goes on to play a major role in the "Plantard plot."

1957: Otto von Habsburg becomes vice-president of the International Paneuropean Union; he serves as president from 1973–2004. The European Economic Community is founded.

1960-65: Second Vatican Council is held in Rome.

1961: Otto von Habsburg renounces his family's long-defunct claim to the Austrian throne; he is active in the European Parliament.

1965: The Inquisition is reorganized and renamed.

1969: A break-in at the Vatican is played down; the P2 Masonic lodge begins to infiltrate the Italian government, the Vatican Bank, and the Mafia.

1970: The Swiss Guard and Vatican police are modernized; two other Vatican guard units are disbanded.

1982: The publication of *The Holy Blood and the Holy Grail* brings worldwide attention to the Plantard plot; the Inquisition possibly takes over Opus Dei.

1998: Vatican authorities allege that the deaths of the Swiss Guard's commander, his wife, and a young guardsman are the result of a love triangle.

1989: The Paneuropean Union organizes "the Paneuropean Picnic" on the Austro-Hungarian border. As a result Hungary opens its borders, beginning the fall of the Iron Curtain.

2003: Publication of *The Da Vinci Code* renews interest in the Plantard plot and brings Opus Dei out of the shadows.

2007: Otto von Habsburg retires and hands over his duties to his son Karl.

2012: The "Vatileaks" scandal exposes financial corruption at the highest levels; the Vatican's internal investigation is headed by a senior member of Opus Dei. Professor Émile Fouchet dies in an apparent car accident near Troyes, France.

Bibliography

Books

There are hundreds of books on Templar secrets in print in English, and many more in French. Each year sees more titles published, many elaborating on existing theories and evidence and a few presenting new ideas and information. The following list cannot be more than a selection.

Addison, Charles G., *The History of the Knights Templars, the Temple Church, and the Temple*, Longman, Brown, Green, and Longmans (London, 1842). Available as a free e-text through Project Gutenberg.

Ambrosini, Maria Luisa, *The Secret Archives of the Vatican*, Little, Brown & Co (New York, 1969).

Baigent, Michael, Richard Leigh, and Henry Lincoln, *The Holy Blood and the Holy Grail*, Jonathan Cape (London, 1982).

Baigent, Michael and Richard Leigh, *The Temple and the Lodge*, Arcade Publishing (New York, 1991).

Bradley, Michael, *Grail Knights of North America: On The Trail of the Grail Legacy in Canada and the United States*, Hounslow Press (Toronto, 1998).

Brown, Dan, *The Da Vinci Code*, Bantam Dell (New York, 2003).

Burman, Edward, *The Inquisition*, Dorset Press (New York, 1992).

Clifton, Chas S., *Encyclopedia of Heresies and Heretics*, Barnes & Noble (New York, 1992).

Cowper, Marcus, *Cathar Castles* (Fortress 55), Osprey Publishing (Oxford, 2006).

Daraul, Arkon, *Secret Societies: A History*, MJF Books (New York, 1989).

Gabrieli, Francesco, *Arab Historians of the Crusades*, Barnes & Noble (New York, 1993).

Haag, Michael, *The Templars: History and Myth*, Profile Books (London, 2009).

Heckethorn, Charles William, *The Secret Societies of All Ages and Countries*, Cosimo Classics (New York, 2005).

Hopkins, Marilyn, and Tim Wallace-Murphy, *Templars in America: From the Crusades to the New World*, Red Wheel/Weiser (Newburyport, MA, 2004).

Keightley, Thomas, *Secret Societies of the Middle Ages*, William Clowes & Sons (London, 1837). Available as a free e-text through Project Gutenberg.

Matarasso, P. M. (trans.), *The Quest of the Holy Grail*, Penguin Books (London, 1969).

McCall, Andrew, *The Medieval Underworld*, A. M. Heath (1979).

Mann, William F., *The Knights Templar in the New World: How Henry Sinclair Brought the Grail to Acadia*, Destiny Books (Rochester, VT, 2004).

Oxbrow, Mark, and Ian Robertson, *Rosslyn and the Grail*, Mainstream Publishing (Edinburgh, 2005).

Index